Emily Dickinson

HER LETTER TO THE WORLD

❧§❧

Emily Dickinson

HER LETTER TO THE WORLD

By Polly Longsworth

❧§❧

THOMAS Y. CROWELL COMPANY   NEW YORK

JB Dickinson Copy 3 54

Acknowledgment is made to the following for permission to use copyrighted material.

The Belknap Press of Harvard University Press for poetry appearing on the following pages, from *The Poems of Emily Dickinson*, edited by Thomas H. Johnson, copyright 1951, 1955 by The President and Fellows of Harvard College: Pages 84, 108, 116, 126 (also Little, Brown and Company); pages viii, 78, 83, 91, 93, 94, 97, 107, 115, 124, 125, 127, 139, 140, 157, 160; and for short excerpts from *The Letters of Emily Dickinson*, edited by Thomas H. Johnson and Theodora V. W. Ward, copyright © 1958 by The President and Fellows of Harvard College, and reprinted by permission of the publishers and the trustees of Amherst College.

Emily Dickinson at times made several variations of the same poem. Other slight variations in her manuscripts were created by well-intentioned editors who published her work over the years. In his volumes, Mr. Johnson has returned to the most original form of each poem and letter, establishing as accurately as possible the text actually written and preferred by Emily Dickinson. The poet's misspellings and her use of dashes as her chief form of punctuation survive in the variations selected by Mr. Johnson and are reprinted intact in this biography.

BOOKS BY THE AUTHOR

Exploring Caves
Emily Dickinson: Her Letter to the World

For Amy
and Elizabeth

This is my letter to the World
That never wrote to Me—
The simple News that Nature told—
With tender Majesty

Her Message is committed
To Hands I cannot see—
For love of Her—Sweet—countrymen—
Judge tenderly—of Me

Emily Dickinson

Prologue

The great valley of the Connecticut River begins in northern New Hampshire, cuts a swath through the western half of Massachusetts, and cleaves the state of Connecticut as the river winds slowly southward to the Atlantic Ocean. The settlers of America early began their movement westward from the coastal regions into the rich, fertile bottomlands along the Connecticut. Hundreds of farming communities had begun prospering by 1700. When the Revolution started, the valley had become, in the words of one commentator upon the scene, "a rich, well cultivated Vale thickly settled and swarming with people."

One of the many communities located in the valley was Amherst, Massachusetts. It was peopled by farmers from the neighboring westerly settlement of Hadley shortly after the menace of Indian wars had passed from the region. Formally founded in 1759, the town was named after Lord Jeffrey Amherst, the general of the British army who fought successfully against the French in the battle for Cape Breton Island in 1758.

Today if one climbs to the top of 950-foot-high Mt.

Holyoke, southwest of Amherst, it is easy to see what attracted the pioneers to the area. The valley spread below is a spectacular sight. Amherst rests on a stretch of rich, flat land that in prehistoric times was the bottom of a great glacial lake. Nature has handsomely framed the flats on all sides. On the east roll the forest-covered Pelham Hills, immediately to the south rise the ancient, abrupt, lava-formed Holyoke Mountains, guarding the north are stumps of still other prehistoric mountains, while on the west coils the serpentine Connecticut River. Originally the green forests of New England stretched in every direction, as far as the eye could see.

Before the Revolutionary War Amherst appeared no different from neighboring farm communities. A traveler to the town would have discovered an inn, a small wooden meetinghouse, and a few dwellings with tilled acreage arrayed around a great marshy common. The common served as pastureland for cows and other grazing animals. The citizens of the town were hard-working farmers who raised the food needed to support their families and who preserved the strong Puritan beliefs they had brought with them from the Atlantic seaboard.

The nineteenth century, following the War for Independence, was a prosperous one for the Connecticut Valley. The fifty years between 1830 and 1880 marked the peak of New England agriculture, and Amherst reflected the general

prosperity of the entire region. By mid-century the population of Amherst had swelled to three thousand, and many
new white clapboard homes had been built around the common and on side streets. The surrounding farms with their
crops of corn, hay, and tobacco had every sign of well-being.
Numerous merchants had opened shops. In the center of
town, beneath the swinging wooden sign of the Boltwood
Tavern, stopped the snorting horses and jolting carriages
of two stagecoach lines, one running north and south from
Brattleboro to Hartford and the other east and west between
Boston and Albany.

But the biggest change in Amherst was a cultural one. It
came about as a result of the intellectual and moral fervor
of some of the citizens of Amherst. These citizens were
merchants, ministers, lawyers, and prosperous farmers of
the town, farsighted and pious men, an unusual number of
whom held degrees from such New England colleges as
Yale and Dartmouth, Harvard and Williams. Their strong
belief in the value of education led to the founding, in 1814,
of the excellent Amherst Academy to educate the boys and
girls of the area.

With another burst of zeal, and with great effort and
sacrifice, some of the same leaders went on to establish
Amherst College for the purpose of educating "indigent
young men of piety and talents for the Christian ministry."
Beginning in 1821 the college buildings rose on the high

ground at the south end of the common, across from the First Congregational Church. Later, in 1863, the Massachusetts Agricultural College was founded at the north end of town. The Agricultural College is today the University of Massachusetts.

To Amherst, then, came the academic life, bringing with it a procession of men and women of cultivated minds and spirits. In addition to being a fairly typical Massachusetts farming community, Amherst became a town whose intellectual climate was stimulating to those who lived there. This undoubtedly accounts for the unusual number of literary figures, from Noah Webster and Helen Hunt Jackson, through Eugene Field and down to Robert Frost, who have been bound up in the town's history.

But the person who most truly belongs to Amherst is the rare, exquisite poet, Emily Dickinson. Born into one of the town's most prominent families, educated at the academy and by her strong associations with the college, she lived her quiet lifetime in one of Amherst's stately tree-shaded homes.

Emily Dickinson's life, from 1830 to 1886, coincides with the period of prosperity in New England. It also spans a time of great change in the ways and thought of its people. By the time she was a mature woman many of the religious strictures, the social customs, and even the literary forms on which she had been nourished as a child had been transformed. In her remarkable poems and letters, which so brilliantly crystallize human experience, Emily Dickinson drew what was purest and most enduring from her Puritan background and from the Amherst environment.

One

The year was 1845. The time, a hot second Thursday in August, and Amherst was astir as it was only once a year, on the day of Amherst College commencement. Inside the crowded First Congregational Meetinghouse a loud burst of applause rose from the seated throng to the high ceilings. As the noise died, the student who had finished speaking was replaced on the platform by another serious, black-robed young man. A quiet, plain-faced girl sitting in the front row of the gallery sat back from the railing and consulted her commencement program.

Josiah Holloway Long of York, New York, eighteenth speaker of the morning, was about to orate upon "The State and Tendency of the Nation."

Emily Dickinson let a small sigh escape her. Instantly she won a reproving glance from her mother, seated on her right, and a light jab in the ribs from her younger sister, Lavinia, on the left. Emily made a face at her sister, but refrained from a whispered retort as silence fell upon the congregation.

Clearly, through the open windows, came the shouting and laughter of people celebrating on the common outside. There wasn't room in the church for the crowd that had poured into town that morning by horse, buggy, or farm wagon to watch the annual commencement parade and, if possible, attend the graduation ceremonies. Emily had caught only a glimpse of the parade this year. Friends and relatives of the graduating seniors had to pass it up and concentrate on getting good seats inside the church if they wanted to hear the program. But from past experience Emily knew the procession was an impressive sight, with the college president, trustees, alumni and students, and even the governor of the Commonwealth of Massachusetts and other special guests marching to the stirring music of the imported Boston Brass Band.

Fully around the town common marched the paraders, ending finally at the doors of the pillared meetinghouse, set atop a prominent knoll. There occurred the usual scramble for seats, but there were not nearly enough to go around. People left outside after the doors closed turned to entertain themselves at tents and booths which had been set up overnight on the common. Vendors sold various goods and trinkets, sweet cider, oysters, gingerbread.

The thought of the food being consumed outdoors made Emily's mouth water. It was already high noon, and a good three hours of speech-making remained before the occupants of the meetinghouse would adjourn to the traditional cold luncheon served after commencement.

The heat was oppressive. Buzzing flies and waving fans made the crowded gallery, where the ladies sat, a source of constant low-keyed bustling. Emily found it hard to concentrate on Josiah Long's involved rhetoric, accompanied as it was by many distracting flourishes of his right arm.

How many hours of her lifetime, Emily wondered, had she spent being edified inside this building? If she had followed all the precepts she had heard within these walls, she would undoubtedly now, at fourteen, be a paragon of virtue. For as long as she could remember she had attended services here every Sunday, unless kept home by illness or bad weather. It must add up to hundreds of hours, just like the hundreds of people here today, and the hundreds of words being spoken, and the hundreds of flies. . . .

Sudden loud applause startled Emily, and she realized

she had been dozing, sitting bolt upright in her seat. She hoped her father, whose stern face she could see among the group of trustees and faculty facing her from the platform, had not noticed her closed eyes. But he probably had, and would speak to her about it later. Edward Dickinson was treasurer of the college, and undertook this duty, like the many others in his disciplined life, with great seriousness. Emily's father was a prominent citizen in Amherst, and she well knew he expected his wife and children to conduct themselves accordingly.

Toward midafternoon commencement drew to a close. Degrees were conferred on the thirty-one graduating seniors by President Hitchcock. The program had been varied by a few thumping tunes from the Boston Brass Band, seated below Emily, and by an amusing "Colloquy" in the form of a play acted by six students. There remained only the valedictory address, twenty-ninth and last event of the day. As young Francis March of Worcester mounted the platform to deliver "God in Science," the audience grew unusually quiet. Even the rustling in the gallery ceased.

Listening to the solemn, dignified words of the student before her, Emily was reminded of the seriousness of purpose of these Amherst seniors. Many of them were planning to become ministers; a few, missionaries to far-off lands. Emily knew well that the hearts and minds of many Amherst people were bound up in Amherst College and in these promising young men.

Only a quarter century before, the townspeople had conceived the daring, exciting, and seemingly impossible plan of beginning a college in Amherst to educate young men for the Christian ministry. That meant the Congregational ministry, of course. The vast sum of money needed to begin the college had been raised by great sacrifice among the people in the region.

The fact that her own grandfather, Samuel Fowler Dickinson, whom Emily could just barely remember, had given all he had to this cause he so strongly promoted, was well known. Several times the work on the first college building had come to a halt because funds had run out. On one such occasion Emily's grandfather had sent some of his own workers up the hill to the building site to continue construction.

Now Francis March was concluding his oration with a sad, solemn farewell. Emily's mother, easily moved to tears, began searching her pocket for a handkerchief to wipe her eyes. Many of the ladies around them were quietly weeping, and perhaps some of the men below, also. Edward Dickinson certainly was not. His humorless expression remained unchanged. But many of the trustees sitting near him, those terrifying men with their burning eyes and profuse chin whiskers, looked sad and almost human. Emily made a mental note to describe them in her next letter to her good friend Abiah Root.

As stately final music swelled from below, Emily stood, secretly stretching cramped leg muscles beneath her long skirts. She watched the academic procession pass beneath the balcony and out of the church into the bright August sunshine.

Despite her intention of writing to Abiah Root at once to describe commencement, it was actually many weeks before Emily put pen to paper. By the end of September memories of the mid-August excitement had faded.

One evening, however, as the early autumn darkness drew the Dickinson family together in the lighted front parlor, Emily felt in just the mood to write a long, rambling epistle to her friend in Feeding Hills. She lit a candle with which to see her way upstairs.

"Going to bed so soon, Emily?" questioned Mrs. Dickinson, looking up from the sewing that covered her lap. She peered over the top of her glasses at her elder daughter.

Emily paused at the doorway. The candle flickered as it caught a draft from the hall.

"I'm going up to write a letter to Abiah, Mama," she explained. "I've owed her one for weeks. Since before commencement."

"Then you'd better say your good-nights, dear," was her mother's answer. "And don't be up late."

Emily recrossed the room to kiss her mother's forehead. She went around the back of her father's tall, straight, wing-backed chair and touched his arm lightly. "Good-night, Father."

Edward Dickinson, surprised, looked up from the legal papers he was studying. "Er . . . a . . . . Emily. Yes. Good-night. Is it so late already?" His fingers reached toward his watch pocket.

"I have a letter to write, Father," she explained.

"Well. Yes. Well, see that you're in bed by nine." He consulted his handsome gold pocket watch. "Don't burn your candle at both ends. You need your sleep. Good-night."

"Yes, Father. Good-night."

Emily waved her hand toward the corner of the room where Lavinia and Austin sat reading on opposite sides of a shawl-covered table. They shared the light of the same oil lamp as they hovered over their books. So engrossed were they both, they barely acknowledged their sister's departure from the room.

Out in the hall, away from the fire-warmed parlor, the house was chilly. But Emily scarcely noticed as she climbed the stairs as gaily as her flickering candle permitted. Her mind was on the events of last year, when Abiah had boarded in Amherst and attended the Amherst Academy, and she and Emily had been best friends. What good times they had had. Together with Sarah Tracy, Abby Wood, and Hatty Merrill they had formed a knot of friends called "The Five." Emily wished this year were the same, but "The Five" had dwindled now to two, herself and Abby, and Emily spent much of her time keeping up a correspondence with her now-absent friends. It was scarcely a chore, considering how she loved to write.

Once in her room she set the candlestick on her writing stand and took from a wooden box her pen and a large blue square of clean paper. She sat on the edge of her chair nibbling the wooden pen top thoughtfully for a moment. Then she started filling the page in a tiny, concise hand.

"Dearest Abiah, As I just glanced at the clock and saw how smoothly the little hands glide over the surface, I could scarcely believe that those self-same little hands had eloped with so many precious moments since I received your affectionate letter, and it was still harder for me to believe that I, who am always boasting of being so faithful a correspondent, should have been guilty of negligence in so long delaying to answer it. . . . You asked me if I was attending school now. I am not. Mother thinks me not able to confine myself to school this term. She had rather I would exercise, and I can assure you I get plenty of that article by staying at home. I am going to learn to make bread to-morrow. So you may imagine me with my sleeves rolled up, mixing flour, milk, salaratus, etc., with a deal of grace. I advise you if you don't know how to make the staff of life to learn with dispatch. I think I could keep house very comfortably if I knew how to cook. But as long as I don't, my knowledge of housekeeping is about of as much use as faith without works, which you know we are told is dead. Excuse my quoting from the Scripture, dear Abiah, for it was so handy in this case I couldn't get along very well without it. Since I wrote you last, the summer is past and gone, and autumn with the sere and yellow leaf is already upon us. I never knew the time to pass so swiftly, it seems to me, as the past summer. I really think some one must have oiled his chariot wheels, for I don't recollect of hearing him pass, and I am sure I should if something had not prevented his chariot wheels from creaking as usual. But I will not expatiate upon him any longer, for I know it is wicked to trifle with so revered a personage, and I fear he will make me a call in person to inquire as to the remarks which I have made concerning him. Therefore I will let him alone for the present. . . . How are you getting on with your music? Well, I hope and trust. I am taking lessons and am getting along very well, and now I have a piano, I am very happy. . . . Have you any flowers now? I have had a beautiful flower-garden this summer; but they are nearly gone now. It is very cold to-night, and I mean to pick the prettiest ones before I go to bed, and cheat Jack Frost of so many of *the treasures* he calculates to rob to-night. Won't it be a capital idea to put him at defiance, for once at least, if no more? I would love to send you a bouquet if I had an opportunity, and you could press it and write under it, The last flowers of summer. Wouldn't it be poetical, and you know that is what young ladies aim to be now-a-days. . . . I expect I have altered a good deal since I have seen you, dear Abiah. I have grown tall a good deal, and wear my golden tresses done up in a net-cap. Modesty, you know, forbids me to mention whether my personal appearance has altered. I leave that for others to judge. But my [word omitted] has not changed, nor will it in time to come. I shall always remain the same old sixpence. . . . I can say no more now, as it is after ten, and everybody has gone to bed but me. Don't forget your affectionate friend,

> Emily E. D."

Emily yawned and stretched. She had gone on writing much longer than she intended. Whatever would Abiah think of so much foolishness, she wondered? And the writing looked so crowded on the page. She envisioned her friend having to peer through a magnifying glass to decipher it.

Emily blotted carefully, then folded the sheet so all the writing was turned to the inside. On a blank area that faced outward she wrote the address, and from a box of stickers and mottos chose a small gilt rectangle which said, "From you know who" to seal the letter.

Emily yawned a second time. What was the other thing on her mind for tonight? She tried to remember. Oh yes, her flowers. After a moment's consideration she decided to let Jack Frost thieve what he would this one night. It was much too late to steal down through the dark house, now locked for the night, to pick the remaining blossoms. Her father would have something to say about such an escapade if he discovered her!

Emily blew out the stub of her candle and shivered as she undressed in the dark. Her bed felt so inviting and her quilt so cozy, she was asleep within two minutes. The Dickinsons' large white house was swallowed in darkness that shrouded the whole valley. No house lights glimmered. There were no street lights. Amherst slept.

Emily had been born in another house in Amherst, the handsome brick Dickinson homestead on Main Street. Early on the wintry morning of December 10, 1830, Dr. Isaac Cutler, trudging wearily home through the snow after a night spent in attendance with Mrs. Edward Dickinson, made this brief entry in his record book for December:

*Edward Dickinson Esq*ʳ *10 G*

Scarcely less succinct, Emily's father added two lines to the family history written on the flyleaf of his Bible:

Emily Elizabeth, their second child was
born Dec. 10. 1830. at 5:o'clock. A.M.

Emily's brother, named William Austin but always called Austin, was already one and one half years old. A third child, Lavinia Norcross, was born when Emily was two. These three, close in age and always to remain unusually close in their interests and their devotion to one another, completed the Dickinson family.

The homestead had been built in 1813 by Emily's grandfather, Samuel Fowler Dickinson. At the time it was the first brick house in Amherst, and townspeople early began calling it The Mansion.

According to Noah Webster, who from 1812 to 1822 lived just up the street from the homestead while beginning work on his famous dictionary, a mansion is a dwelling with four chimneys. The Dickinson house had five. In addition, the grounds contained a barn, carriage shed, large woodpile, and a profusion of shrubs and trees. From their front windows the Dickinsons looked across the dirt highway leading to Boston to their wide, hay-filled meadow. Beyond they caught a glimpse of the adjacent Pelham Hills.

Emily was born into a busy household, for her parents were sharing the homestead with her Grandmother and

Grandfather Dickinson and numerous aunts and uncles. The early 1830's was a low point in the fortunes of the family. Samuel Fowler Dickinson had been so involved in the movement that founded Amherst College during the preceding decade that he had given it almost everything he had. He had given freely of time and money in support of other causes as well, with the result that his law practice had dwindled and he was nearly penniless.

While respected as a great and good man in Amherst, Emily's grandfather was forced to leave the town in 1833 to take a position at Lane Seminary in Ohio. He died, a broken man, in Hudson, Ohio, five years later.

Before leaving Amherst, Emily's grandfather sold the western half of the homestead, where he had raised his nine children, to Deacon David Mack. When Emily was nine her father sold his part of the property to Deacon Mack also and moved his family to a big white wooden house on North Pleasant Street.

The burden of his father's failure can only have strengthened the already strong character of Edward Dickinson. Left in the early stages of his career with an almost nonexistent law practice and no money, he had to his credit the Dickinson integrity and a degree from Yale College in New Haven, Connecticut. With these he set about rebuilding his fortune.

Edward Dickinson steered clear of flighty idealism. He

was a practical man through and through, although not
without great interest in civic enterprises. He shortly became
treasurer of Amherst College, a position he held for over
thirty years. He became a staunch member of the Whig
party, served in the state legislature and, for a short time,
as a member of Congress. He supported the Temperance
Association, contributed frequently to the local newspaper,
and led the fight to bring the railroad to Amherst. In short,
for four decades there was scarcely a worthy project or organ-
ization in Amherst that did not know Edward Dickinson
as one of its leading forces. At the end of his life he was
recalled as "a rock of faithfulness and integrity through
every crisis." Meanwhile he built up a good law practice
and became known as Squire Dickinson.

You might suppose that a man of high seriousness, great
strength of character and firmness of purpose, capable of
vigorous dedication to duty would be a little difficult to live
with. He was.

Emily's father was said to "lean away from his emotions."
He seldom laughed, rarely expressed his devotion to his wife
and children. Yet he was not entirely humorless, and he
deeply loved his family. He was stern and unbending and,
to at least one acquaintance, appeared "thin, dry & speech-
less." But his children, although they feared him when they
were young, and struggled to assert their independence of
him as young men and women, loved him and learned to

live with him as they matured. He became the keystone of their lives.

The bond between Emily and her father grew particularly strong as the years passed. As a child she trembled at his strictness. Once she told a friend, "I never knew how to tell time by the clock till I was fifteen. My father thought he had taught me but I did not understand and I was afraid to say I did not and afraid to ask anyone else, lest he should know."

But from the time she was twenty-two her father would eat bread baked only by Emily, and when she was twenty-eight she declined an invitation to visit a friend, explaining, "I do not go out at all, lest Father will come and miss me, or miss some little act, which I might forget, should I run away."

Edward Dickinson kept his family close around him all his life, but he never let down the barriers to his own heart and soul. Emily later said, "His Heart was pure and terrible and I think no other like it exists." And Austin, as a man of forty-five, leaned over his father's casket to kiss the dead man's face, saying, "There, father, I never dared do that while you were living."

Every weekday morning of his adult life Squire Dickinson punctually strode along the dirt sidewalk from his home to his law office in the center of town. Dressed in black broadcloth, with a tall gray beaver hat rising above his stern countenance, Squire Dickinson looked every inch the leading citizen he was, and he must have struck terror into the heart of many a small boy who passed him.

The woman Edward Dickinson chose for his wife was almost his opposite in character. He met Emily Norcross while he was at Yale and she at boarding school in New Haven. She was quiet, meek, and, once married, became greatly dependent upon the advice and direction of her strong-minded husband. All her energies were devoted to the tasks of keeping house and raising children, no small undertaking in that time, and she let her husband deal with any issues outside the confinements of domestic routine.

Life in the Dickinson household was generally close and harmonious, though much more formal than the home life we are accustomed to today. While Austin, Emily, and Lavinia tended to take after their strong-minded father rather than their more ineffectual mother, they were loving, obedient, and respectful to both parents, as children were trained to be. Father guided their behavior diligently. They were well aware of what was right and wrong.

The winter Emily was seven Edward Dickinson was in Boston serving in the state legislature. His advice continued to flow freely in his frequent letters:

". . . I want to have you do perfectly right—always be kind & pleasant, & always tell the truth, & never deceive.

That is the way to become good. . . . I want to have you grow up & become good men & women—and learn all you can, so that you can teach others to do right. You have enough to eat & drink, & good clothes—& go to school— while a great many poor little children have to go hungry— and have ragged clothes—& sleep cold, & have poor green wood to burn, & can't have books or go to school. All you learn, now, when you are young, will do you a great deal of good, when you are grown up. . . ."

Outside the walls of her home Emily's life was guided by the Church, by her school, and by her relationships with the people who lived in the small, self-sufficient village and who were interdependent upon one another for their thought, work, entertainment, and way of life.

Two

Edward Dickinson sat stiffly on the embroidered seat of a straight-backed chair, his back to the east windows. Fresh, strong spring sunlight flooded into the room from behind him, so that Emily, facing her father from across the parlor, saw him almost silhouetted against the brilliance.

With the family Bible spread open upon his knees, Mr. Dickinson was conducting his family's morning devotions. His wife and children were seated quietly and attentively before him in their accustomed chairs. Outdoors the birds sang lustily. Their song did not register upon the ear of

Edward Dickinson, but it seemed fairly to deafen his elder daughter. Every bird in creation must be rejoicing in the beauty of this morning, thought Emily. Even the pattern of shadows rippling over the carpets at her feet spoke gay though silent contrast to the solemn biblical text she listened to.

"Let us hear the conclusion of the whole matter," read Edward Dickinson from Ecclesiastes. "Fear God, and keep his commandments: for this is the whole duty of man. For God shall bring every work into judgement, and every secret thing, whether it be good or whether it be evil."

The passage was as familiar to Emily as any nursery rhyme. This morning, however, it seemed specially chosen to rebuke her for the pleasure she was taking in the glorious spring day. It reminded her of the past winter, which she preferred now not to think of, when through several months of inner turmoil she had wrestled with the problem of becoming a Christian.

For as long as Emily could remember she had devoted the seventh day of every week of her life to God. Twice each Sabbath she sat through services in the family pew at First Church, listening to such passages from the Bible as her father was reading this morning. When she and Austin and Vinnie were small enough that their high-buttoned boots swung short of the carpeted prayer cushions, the Bible's fire and brimstone flew round their heads in the most bewilder-

ing way. God was an image, an all-seeing eye somewhere
up above the creosote-dripping heating pipes. His power
was somehow represented in the children's minds by deep
Judgement-Day chords from the bass viol, the instrument
that accompanied the gloomy hymns.

As she grew older the message of the Bible became
clearer. Along with poetic passages, Emily absorbed Congregational Church doctrine, learning that in order to be
chosen by God for immortal life she must first acknowledge
herself a Christian and thereby become a member of the
Church. One was not born a Christian; one became a Christian by receiving inner evidence of God's redeeming grace.
An individual's duty lay in leading a life of spiritual righteousness and readiness to acknowledge the Lord.

A revival of religious fervor gripped Amherst College and
the congregations of many churches in the Amherst area
during the winter Emily was fifteen. At first she was caught
up in it, as were such friends as Abby Wood, and Abiah
Root in Feeding Hills. Emily first experienced despondency
born of the recognition of her own sinfulness. This was
followed by a period of ecstasy during which she prayed
and resolved to live a godly life. But Emily soon passed
from this state into one of indifference without experiencing
anything she could call evidence of God's grace. She was
far from unmoved by her experience, however, as she confessed in unhappy letters to Abiah.

Sometimes when she looked at her father Emily thought of what a God-fearing man he was. He lived a pious life, while in his soul he silently wrestled with conversion. But he did not yet call himself a Christian, nor join the church he had attended as regularly as clockwork all his life. If Edward Dickinson set such high standards for his soul, who was Emily to presume?

The experience was behind her now. This beautiful June morning in 1846 could not be spoiled by memories of the winter. As Squire Dickinson summoned his family to its knees, Emily abandoned any effort to keep her mind on the devotions. She ached to be outdoors and on her way to school, but her father had selected this particular morning for an absolutely endless prayer. Emily pictured the whole family still kneeling there twenty years hence, listening to the same prayer which had never reached an amen. Her mother and father would be white-haired. Austin would have grown chin whiskers. And Lavinia—Emily caught herself from giggling—Vinnie would have burst out of her dress. Every seam would have given way. Such an imagined indignity to her sister's vanity struck Emily as very funny.

Mr. Dickinson rumbled on. ". . . And we ask in conclusion, almighty Father, thy blessing on these thy servants, gathered here, that we may walk in thy ways and praise thee evermore, saying: 'Our Father which art in heaven, Hallowed be thy name . . . ' "

The voices of Mrs. Dickinson, Austin, Emily, and Lavinia joined his in repeating the Lord's Prayer, and their
worship service was at last over. The room came suddenly
to life as Edward Dickinson raised himself to his feet and
replaced the large Bible on the shelf beside the mantel.

Austin, suddenly very tall, seemed to fill the house as he
strode here and there collecting books and papers, demand-
ing of his mother whether he could expect roast chicken
for dinner, tweaking the bow of Vinnie's apron as he passed
her. When he finally took his cap from the rack in the hall
and gave the front door a resounding, knocker-thumping
bang, the house seemed to take a deep breath.

Austin was preparing to enter Amherst College in the
fall, and in Emily's eyes, as well as his own, he appeared to
be gaining enormously in stature. Emily looked up to him
now more than ever. She loved to match wits with him at
the dinner table, across the stern and somewhat disapprov-
ing countenance of their father.

Edward Dickinson, too, was gathering his legal briefs,
his gold-headed walking stick, and his high beaver hat.
Father's leave-taking was quieter and more methodical than
Austin's, and no door-slamming was to be expected when
he left the house. With his hand on the big brass knob he
looked back to say, "Emily. There is something I wish to
discuss with you this evening."

With her? What could it be? Had she been misbehaving

again? Questions and speculations sped rapidly through Emily's head as she replied a simple "Yes, Father." Formal discussions between Edward Dickinson and his children usually signified some important change. In Emily's case the change seemed most often to concern her conduct. Father on occasion thought her willful and stubborn and took her to task for it.

Mr. Dickinson closed the front door firmly behind him. Emily returned from hall to parlor to find Lavinia absorbed in patting her hair before the mirror. Vinnie cautiously turned her head this way and that to gauge the effect. How handsome her sister was growing these days, thought Emily with a tiny wince. Certainly the gap between her own big-eyed plainness and Vinnie's soft prettiness was more and more noticeable. What had become noticeable to her parents, too, was Vinnie's obvious pleasure in her appearance, and more than once her father had had to counsel her about vainness. Emily knew Vinnie would never dare primp so openly if Edward Dickinson were still in the house.

Mrs. Dickinson was busily fussing about the parlor with the feather duster in one hand and a pitcher of water for the geraniums in the other. She kissed her daughters a preoccupied good-bye and bustled off to the kitchen. The hired girl would by now have cleared breakfast away and would be ready to begin the morning's many projects.

"Goodness, Lavinia," said Emily impatiently. "Part with

the looking glass! We'll be late for school if we don't hurry!"

Unperturbed, Vinnie adjusted her shawl and gave herself a final pat before she trailed Emily from the room. Upon opening the front door the girls were met by a burst of sunlight. For a moment they stood on the small portico, blinking like cats in the warm brilliance. The blossoms of a bleeding heart growing beside the steps trembled in a gentle breeze. A bird sang lustily from the blooming magnolia. Beyond the young orchard, sun glittered on the granite headstones of the village cemetery and, farther off, bathed the new green of the Pelham Hills. Emily and Vinnie breathed deeply of spring-scented air. Then, opening the front gate, they fairly skipped down North Pleasant Street to the academy.

Their destination was a three-story brick building, painted white, which stood on a slight rise on Amity Street, just west of the center of town. The spring term was only a week old, but already Emily was enjoying it immensely. She loved her subjects and, as always, she loved her teacher. To make everything perfect, this term her favorite teacher, Miss Elizabeth Adams, was back as preceptress after an absence of more than a year.

The school bell began to ring its final warning as Vinnie and Emily cut catty-corner across Amherst's main intersection. Skirts flying, netted hair bobbing, they scurried as quickly as their book-filled arms would permit. Past the

Amherst House and its carriage shed they ran, to arrive breathless at the school door just in time to slip into two empty seats in the academy hall before morning prayers began.

Emily's education had begun in the West Middle District public school, a plain, two-story brick building almost directly across the street from where she now lived. There she had learned to read, write, and cipher along with dozens of other children of varying ages, all sharing the same large plain room and the same teacher.

When she was eleven Emily's father entered her in the Amherst Academy. There, by her own admission, occurred the happiest times of her youth. At the academy she was well-grounded in Latin, mathematics, history, and geography. She also studied mental and natural philosophy, ecclesiastical history, and a wide selection of sciences. Botany stimulated in her a love of flowers that lasted all her life. With her friends she took long rambles in the fields and woods collecting wildflowers to bring home and press in her herbarium. She cultivated her own flower garden in summertime and tended a stand of potted plants during the winter.

But Emily could not easily have ignored the science of geology. Dr. Hitchcock, president of the college and professor of geology, had made dramatic, original discoveries about the valley in which Amherst was situated. He advanced the theory that the broad, fertile Connecticut Valley had, in prehistoric times, been a vast lake formed by melting water from the last Ice Age glacier. Poking about on ledges of the nearby Holyoke Range, Edward Hitchcock found hundreds of fossilized dinosaur tracks left still earlier by Triassic giants who had roamed the basin's firm clays. The college museums which housed his specimens were for decades a feature attraction for visitors to the town. Academy students studying geology were permitted to attend Dr. Hitchcock's lectures.

A regular part of the academy curriculum was an exercise known as speaking and composition. Every Wednesday afternoon the students were required to read aloud to classmates a paper written during the preceding two weeks. Emily loved writing compositions. They challenged her growing wit and originality. She cared less for reading or reciting aloud. Her natural shyness caused her great discomfort. Rhetoric received such emphasis among the students at both school and college level, however, that reciting in public was an experience she was forced to endure as long as she attended school.

Emily, who early had an ear for the ridiculous, reported on one of her early speaking and composition exercises:

"This Afternoon is Wednesday and so of course there was Speaking and Composition—there was one young man who read a Composition the Subject was think twice before you speak—he was describing the reasons why any one should do so—one was—if a young gentleman—offered a young lady his arm and he had a dog who had no tail and he boarded at the tavern think twice before you speak . . . he is the sillyest creature that ever lived I think. I told him that I thought he had better think twice before he spoke."

Emily enjoyed school. Her quick, retentive mind partook eagerly of what was offered, and her enthusiasm for her subjects, her books, and her teachers was boundless. Unfortunately, poor health kept her from attending as regularly as she would have liked. The school year was divided into four terms of eleven weeks, with two weeks of vacation between. It was a system that tolerated irregular attendance, for each term formed a complete block of study. If sickness kept Emily at home during the spring, she could return to school for new courses the following term.

Squire Dickinson kept sharp watch on Emily's constitution. If a cough persisted or a period of melancholy lingered, she was kept out of school until her condition improved. During such periods she concentrated at home on exercise, piano lessons, occasional language and singing lessons, and such ladylike pursuits as knitting edging, working slippers, and stitching bookmarks.

In an age when dust and dirt were tackled with broom,

elbow grease, and water hauled from the well, and cooking a meal began with killing the fowl and fetching wood for the stove, housekeeping was a detailed and endless occupation. Emily and Vinnie had duties they were expected to perform. Guests arrived frequently and were likely to stay for long visits, so there was always plenty for every member of the family to do.

A hired girl employed indoors and a hired man outdoors helped the Dickinsons with their heavier household chores. The vegetable garden must be hoed, the apples, peaches, pears, cherries, and grapes that grew on the Dickinson property must be tended in season. The care and feeding of poultry seems to have been Austin's job, egg-gathering was likely Emily and Vinnie's. Austin's chores included bringing in water from the well and wood from the woodpile for the stoves and fireplaces. Wood was the only fuel used to heat the big house. Edward Dickinson was said to keep the biggest woodpile in town, a fact that undoubtedly was a matter of both pride and anguish for his son.

On the afternoon of the June day in 1846 that Emily and Vinnie were almost late for school, lessons eventually came to an end. When the principal had said a last benediction on the day and the school bell had pronounced by vigorous clanging the end of classes, Emily left the building arm in arm with Abby Wood among a throng of students.

The air was still lovely, still clear and sparkling, as if the morning freshness had determined to spend the day. Later in the summer, drought and dust from the plowed fields would combine to turn the town a different color. Buildings and grass areas edging the dirt roads would be coated gray by passing carriage wheels. Ladies' skirts would raise little clouds as they swept along. But rain had been plentiful this spring, and now, cool, lush greenness of tree and meadow met the eye in every direction.

"Oh, Abby, it's so beautiful!" exclaimed Emily to her best friend. "This day wasn't meant to be spent indoors!"

"Let's not, then," replied Abby. "I was thinking this morning that it must be time for the Indian pipes to be up."

Abby hit a responsive chord in Emily, who loved to pick the wildflowers that grew in abundant variety around Amherst. The year before when she and Abby were searching for fringed gentians they had unexpectedly found a patch of delicate plants with white, leafless stems and shy, bowed heads standing small and slender atop the shaded bank of a damp ravine. There seemed something so courageous in the isolated purity of Indian pipes that the girls had not touched them. But Emily wanted to try transplanting the little flowers to a dark corner of her own garden.

"I'm sure you're right," Emily agreed with her friend wistfully. "But I can't go today. I have to practice until suppertime. Why don't we go on Saturday? Let's do, Abby! And look for the early lilies and pitcher plants, too."

But Abby would not give up her friend so easily. "At least walk with me across the common, Emily," she begged. "You haven't for ages. The piano won't run away."

Emily acquiesced, and arm in arm the girls crossed the road to the wide, grassy common. This long stretch of pasture formed the center of town. Six rods wide and partially fenced, it was bordered on the north and west by the business buildings of Amherst. Among these Cutler's Drygoods Store sold everything from bonnet silk to paint and groceries, and Mr. Pierce's Shoe Store advertised ladies' lasting gaiters and velvet shoes. Farther down the west side of the common, and on the east as well, were handsome white clapboard houses, many surrounded by neat picket fences, that composed a setting typical of many prosperous New England villages.

The common itself, however, was uneven and unsightly. Its northern end was very marshy, and on summer evenings the sound of peepers was almost deafening. Occasionally animals grazed on the higher ground, and geese flocked here and there. A wooden rail fence surrounded the entire northern end; the southern common was higher and drier and unfenced. In the early spring, melting snow and ice turned the center of town into an almost impassable muddy bog. Amherst College students tramping about in the March and April muck complained of the danger of losing their boots.

There was no mud this June day, however. Abby and Emily skirted the western edge of the common until they reached the little footpath leading across. High grass tickled their stockinged ankles. Daisies and dandelions, clover and buttercups, spotted the unkempt carpet. Here and there a patch of blue stargrass twinkled at them, and butterflies and bumblebees flew from clump to clump of sundrenched flowers.

Beyond the homes on the common, fields and groves of primeval trees beckoned Emily and Abby. The sweet scents, the thousand tiny sounds of early summer, wooed their senses. Emily longed to take a late afternoon ramble, but her sense of duty prevailed. She was committed to two hours of piano practice each day. There was the table to lay for tea, her lessons to do for the next day. She said good-bye to Abby and sought to exorcise her energy and high spirits by running the full length of the common back to the center of town.

Emily had been practicing long and hard. The martial notes of "The Lancers Quickstep" swelled from the piano and filled the whole downstairs, so that Mrs. Dickinson, preparing supper in the kitchen, fairly trotted to the melody as she moved from sink to woodstove to kitchen table. Absorbed in her music, Emily did not hear her father come in, and his hand on her shoulder startled her.

"Forgive me, Emily," her father apologized. "I didn't mean to frighten you. I just thought you might stop now to have that talk I mentioned this morning. It seems a good time."

Her father looked serious, but since he always did, Emily could not discern from his face how far she had strayed from the path of righteousness this time. She moved from the piano bench to the edge of the sofa, facing her father's favorite chair. Their interviews were always conducted in this manner.

"Emily," began Edward Dickinson, crossing one leg over the other. "Your mother and I are aware of your industry in your schoolwork. It pleases us that you have applied yourself in the courses you have taken and that you seem eager to improve your mind."

Emily was bewildered. She had not expected the conversation to take such a positive course, for her father was rarely vocal in his approval of any of his children. What could he be leading to?

"You are aware, as we are, that you are not strong in health," continued Mr. Dickinson, seemingly on another tack. "When you indulge in too many activities at once the overstimulation taxes you badly." He paused. "However, if your health should not in any way be endangered, and if you should wish it, we would like you to prepare yourself to enter Mount Holyoke Seminary in another year."

She was stunned. Her thoughts whirled this way and that off the axis of her brain. Mount Holyoke Seminary in South Hadley . . . in her wildest dreams . . . live away from home . . . but the entrance examinations . . . leave her dear family . . . a student of Mary Lyon. She collected herself long enough to say fervently, "Oh, Father, yes! I *would* like to try!"

Did he really mean it? That she could go the ten miles over the Holyoke Mountains to attend the seminary? It seemed he did. Edward Dickinson referred briefly to a theme he had dwelt upon before, that his father's counsel had always been to educate one's daughters as well as one's sons, then the interview seemed to be at an end.

Emily wondered shyly if she might kiss her father to express her gratitude. Instinct would have led her to throw her arms around his neck. But nothing in Edward Dickinson's countenance or bearing invited such abandon. He merely said flatly, "The next four terms at the academy will be devoted to preparing you for Mount Holyoke. We shall select your courses with care."

Of course. And she would work harder than she had ever worked before, Emily promised herself. Her love for books had purpose now. At the moment the urge to share her news was her strongest impulse. Whom should she tell? Whom *could* she tell? For all her sober appearance as she followed her father from the parlor, Emily was dancing inside. Austin surely would share her pleasure, and Vinnie, too. But the need to pour out her joy upon paper found expression before many days had passed in a letter to Abiah. How different it was from her last few letters in which she had brooded about the state of her soul. In June she wrote rapidly in her concise, fine penmanship:

"It seems to me that time has never flown so swiftly with me as it has the last spring. I have been busy every minute, and not only so, but hurried all the time. So you may imagine that I have not had a spare moment, much though my heart has longed for it, to commune with an absent friend. . . . I presume you will be wondering by this time what I am doing to be in so much haste as I have declared myself to be. Well, I will tell you. I am fitting to go to South Hadley Seminary, and expect if my health is good to enter that institution a year from next fall. Are you not astonished to hear such news? You cannot imagine how much I am anticipating in entering there. It has been in my thought by day, and my dreams by night, ever since I heard of South Hadley Seminary. I fear I am anticipating too much, and that some freak of fortune may overturn all my airy schemes for future happiness. But it is my nature always to anticipate more than I realize."

Three

The road over the Hol-
yoke Mountains from Amherst to South Hadley was ten
miles long. It left the Amherst common and passed the
meadows and fields of farmers living south of town. Before
long the landscape changed from open land to woods, so
that tree-covered slopes formed the principal view of the
occupants of the passing Dickinson buggy. With Edward
Dickinson holding the reins and Emily perched on the seat
beside him, the open vehicle rolled up and through the
Notch between two mountains, then along the hillsides on
the far side toward Mount Holyoke Female Seminary.

It was late September of 1847, and night frosts had already set a few sugar maples ablaze. The vibrant spectacle of a New England autumn was just beginning. Emily had ample opportunity to view it during the hour and a half she traveled the country road.

But she had far more than landscapes on her mind this particular morning. Although she sat quietly, with her hands joined in her lap, her heart was fluttering nervously inside and her throat felt full. She had just endured a sad and tremulous leave-taking from her dear family and beloved home. Ahead lay a new experience, a long year to be spent among strangers at Mount Holyoke.

Emily was apprehensive. Rumors and scraps of information about the lives of the young ladies at the seminary had been forming a crazy-quilt impression in her mind. She would have to wash floors before breakfast, clean gridirons after supper, she had heard. The girls did all their own housekeeping and cooking. There might not be enough to eat. It might not even be palatable.

As soon as she arrived Emily would plunge into the dreaded entrance examinations. She hoped she was prepared. If she failed, or if she could not do the work in the allotted time, Emily knew she would be traveling right back over these mountains in only a few days.

What would her classmates be like? Some claimed that the seminary girls were crude and uncultured. Would she love her new teachers as much as those at the academy? And what about Mary Lyon herself? Austin said the school's preceptress was known among the Amherst College boys as a she-dragon!

The long ride over the rough dirt road began to tire Emily. She was suffering from a bad cold. She had hoped to be rid of it before today, but a harsh cough persisted. Sewing clothes, packing, and saying good-bye to Amherst friends had made the past few weeks unusually busy. Night after night, excitement and anticipation had kept her tossing and turning in her bed long after she was usually asleep. Now that she was actually on her way to Mount Holyoke, Emily realized she was greatly fatigued.

Her father said little during the journey, but stared ahead over the horse's broad chestnut back. Emily was grateful for his silence, although she knew not many days would pass before he wrote her a letter filled with the advice he was now mulling over in his mind. Emily wondered shyly if her father would miss her. Her going left a space in the family circle, an empty chair at mealtime. She suspected, although she would never know, that it also caused an emptiness in Edward Dickinson's heart. It was characteristic of all the Dickinsons that they hated being away from home and from each other. Emily was prepared to endure a bout of homesickness once her father had deposited her in her new surroundings.

After a long, gradual descent from the Notch, the carriage wheels ground around a final curve, and they were at last in South Hadley. The village was smaller than Amherst, and the seminary stood plainly in view on the left side of the road. It was a large red brick building, five stories high, with a two-storied wooden portico across the front. Tall chimneys and a large cupola were visible on the roof. A low white picket fence hemmed the front grounds, and before that stood a row of young elms lifting branches still bearing green leaves.

Edward Dickinson stopped the carriage and helped his daughter step down. She smoothed her dress and rearranged her woolen shawl while she waited for her father to take down the lightest traveling bag. Then, together, Edward and Emily Dickinson, the one figure tall and straight and purposeful, the other small, slim, and hesitant, mounted the wooden steps and rang the bell of the seminary.

The door was opened at once by a plain-faced, simply dressed girl who ushered them in with a smile. Emily and her father stepped into a large parlor furnished with benches and chairs. Rising from among a seated group of people at the far end of the room was a woman who could be no other than Mary Lyon herself. As she came forward to welcome the new arrivals Emily swiftly regarded her from top to toe. She scarcely looked like a she-dragon. Emily intended to set straight her opinionated brother. How could this grandmotherly woman with light auburn hair and sad, though direct, blue eyes, be anything but kind? The lines of Miss Lyon's face looked resolute, yet her voice as she spoke was pleasant, and her words of greeting were hospitable. Emily felt slightly awed by her and said little, letting Miss Lyon and her father talk together.

A moment later Emily was caught up in the normal confusions of arrival. She met Miss Lyon's assistant, Miss Whitman, a young woman with a severe face and hair pulled tightly back into a knot. Several of the teachers and a host of smiling, chattering girls introduced themselves, while a pretty, dark-haired student took Emily to the top floor to find her room. By the time her baggage was settled on the fifth floor and she had said good-bye to her father and watched the dear, familiar horse and buggy disappear down the road, Emily was emotionally and physically exhausted. She stood dejectedly before the parlor window, turning only when she heard a quiet step behind her. It was Miss Lyon.

"Emily," said the school's preceptress. "Is this the first time you have been away from home?"

Emily nodded. "Yes, Miss Lyon. Except for a month in Boston last fall."

"You aren't alone, my dear. Several of our girls have left their dear families for the first time." Mary Lyon smiled gently at her new pupil. "But I feel the adjustment will be a happy one. I don't think of us as a school, you know, but as a large family, living together and working for the glory of God."

Emily nodded again, her eyes downcast. She couldn't think of any reply. Mary Lyon seemed to her an extraordinary creature, somehow elevated from the plane on which other people lived and moved and had their being.

"I feel strongly, Emily, that it is important for all of us to decide now, in the beginning of the year, that we will be cheerful and contented here. It has always been my belief that people who permit themselves to be homesick are wanting in character."

Emily looked up quickly. Miss Lyon's eyes still looked kindly and sad, but Emily saw in them a strength of purpose she had not noticed before. This woman had very definite opinions about right and wrong. Emily, too, had a will of her own. Could she have met a match?

Mary Lyon's next gesture took Emily by surprise. Sympathizing with Emily's obvious unhappiness, and perhaps sensing the fatigue beneath it, Miss Lyon suggested that her new student put off attempting the examinations until the following day. Emily was grateful for the unexpected kindness. She accepted Miss Lyon's proposal with thanks and spent the afternoon resting and unpacking in her tiny room.

The next few days were filled every minute with the new and the different and the unexpected. Emily finished her examinations in three days, finding them no worse than she expected. To her joy she need not face the shame of being sent home for insufficient preparation, as happened to several of the new students. Emily was placed temporarily in the junior, or youngest, class in order to review several subjects. She hoped to enter the middle class at the end of the first term. Once her examinations were finished, and despite Miss Lyon's warning, Emily succumbed to a wretched spell of homesickness.

But before long she began to enjoy Mount Holyoke as much as she could enjoy any place which was not home. For her roommate she had her cousin Emily Norcross of Monson, Massachusetts, a quiet, practical girl who possessed an abundant supply of the shoeblacking Emily Dickinson had never thought to bring from home. Among the other 233 students she found many she liked, although none who could take the place of Abby Wood and a few other close friends at home.

The other girls grew fond of Emily Dickinson. While shy upon first meeting, Emily would warm to people with whom she felt at home, becoming gay and fun-loving. She could tell stories in the most amusing manner, for she had a quick eye for the odd or the ridiculous. Her memory for

quotations and her ability to concoct absurd nonsense entirely out of her head made her conversation and her compositions sparkle.

The dreaded domestic duties turned out to be light,
Emily's consisting of clearing dirty forks from a tier of
dining-hall tables twice a day and washing the same number
after dinner. Beyond that, the girls washed and ironed their
own clothes and took care of their rooms. The food was
surprisingly good, to judge by a menu Emily sent her
brother which listed roast veal, gravy, potatoes, vegetable,
and apple dumpling for the day's dinner. Liquid refresh-
ment was less varied. Nothing stronger than water was
ever served.

The days were full, and no minute went unused. Emily
recorded her schedule for Abiah, who was attending Miss
Campbell's School in nearby Springfield and would appre-
ciate such information:

"At 6. oclock, we all rise. We breakfast at 7. Our study
hours begin at 8. At 9. we all meet in Seminary Hall, for
devotions. At 10¼. I recite a review of Ancient History,
in connection with which we read Goldsmith & Grimshaw.
At .11. I recite a lesson in 'Pope's Essay on Man' which is
merely transposition. At .12. I practice Calisthenics & at
12¼ read until dinner, which is at 12½ & after dinner,
from 1½ until 2 I sing in Seminary Hall. From 2¾ until

3¾. I practise upon the Piano. At 3¾ I go to Sections, where we give in all our accounts for the day, including, Absence—Tardiness—Communications—Breaking Silent Study hours—Receiving Company in our rooms & ten thousand other things, which I will not take time or place to mention. At 4½. we go into Seminary Hall, & receive advice from Miss Lyon in the form of a lecture. We have Supper at 6. & silent-study hours from then until the retiring bell, which rings at 8¾, but the tardy bell does not ring until 9¾, so that we dont often obey the first warning to retire."

Despite such constant activity Emily steadily missed her Amherst family and friends. The highlights of her days were the letters brought from the post office or carried back and forth between Amherst and South Hadley by friends and acquaintances. Better still were the visits from Austin and, occasionally, from Mr. and Mrs. Dickinson. Sometimes they were unexpected, but more often eagerly anticipated. When Austin appeared on a Saturday or Wednesday afternoon he sometimes brought Vinnie or Abby or another young lady with him, not to mention fruit, pies, cakes, and other attentions from home. The young people would sit in one of the parlors and talk, or else tour the building guided by one of the teachers. They could walk in the environs of South Hadley, visiting Young Niagara, a pretty water-wheel falls at a nearby mill, or could ride in the carriage down to view the Connecticut River.

Emily, with her frequent visitors, had more contact with the outside world than many of the students and teachers. Yet even she felt that the seminary family was largely cut off from the events of the world. A month after her arrival at the school she beseeched her brother:

"Wont you please to tell me when you answer my letter who the candidate for President is? I have been trying to find out ever since I came here & have not yet succeeded. I dont know anything more about affairs in the world, than if I was in a trance, & you must imagine with all your 'Sophomoric discernment,' that it is but little & very faint. Has the Mexican war terminated yet & how? Are we beat? Do you know of any nation about to besiege South Hadley? If so, do inform me of it, for I would be glad of a chance to escape, if we are to be stormed. I suppose Miss Lyon. would furnish us all with daggers & order us to fight for our lives, in case such perils should befall us."

On the morning of the day before Thanksgiving Emily woke before dawn and lay listening to the steady, dreary drum of heavily falling rain. When she remembered what day it was, she cast sleep aside impatiently and hopped from her warm bed to the cold, rugless floor, for once paying no attention to the chill that shocked her feet.

"Emily, get up! It's time!" she urged the dim huddled form of her roommate in the other bed. She lit the oil lamp. With noisy splashing and a crash that almost cost her the water pitcher, she poured cold water into the wash bowl and hastily scooped it to her face.

She was not the only girl awake. Throughout the fifth floor the sounds of early morning preparation came from several of the small bedrooms that lined the dark hallway.

"Emily, hurry!" This time Emily Dickinson touched her sleeping cousin's shoulder. "We must be ready."

"What's wrong?" came the muffled reply from the blankets. "Has the bell rung?"

"Not yet. But it will soon. And we have to be ready when Austin comes."

"Emily Dickinson! It's not even six o'clock yet?" An indignant, protesting Emily Norcross sat up in bed and tried unsuccessfully to hunch the blanket around her shoulders.

"It's almost six. Do you want to be late?" By now Emily had donned all her clothing as far as her shift and was about to put over her head the navy-blue wool dress so neatly laid out the night before.

"But he's not coming till after his classes," wailed Emily Norcross. "He won't be here until eleven." Nevertheless she began to worm one large warm foot from under the covers and stretch it toward the floor. Thus she began her usual painful, inch-by-inch emergence from the narrow bed.

Watching her, Emily Dickinson was reminded of one of Miss Lyon's favorite, character-building maxims, "When you know it is time to rise, do it at once." Someday, Emily decided, she would embroider the message into a sampler and hang it over her cousin's bed. This morning Emily Norcross' methodical ways were exasperating.

"Is everything in your traveling bag?" Emily Dickinson inquired to hurry her.

"Of course not!" retorted her cousin, awake enough now to be bad-humored. "I haven't put but my best dress and shoes in yet. What's happened here by the wash stand? There's cold water all over the floor!"

Emily Dickinson was scarcely listening. Today she was going home! Excitement churned in the pit of her stomach. After six long weeks away from Amherst she would have four days of Thanksgiving vacation with her family. No one knew how longingly she had waited for this day. Emily Norcross was spending the vacation with her, and Austin had promised to fetch them both as early as he could.

By the time the six o'clock bell rang Emily was completely dressed and packed, her bed was made, and her part of the room was tidied. She left her roommate fumbling with her shoebuttons and wandered down the hall to see how various friends were faring.

A few girls had so far to travel they left before breakfast, and their empty places in the large basement dining hall added to the unusual atmosphere of the morning. After breakfast the normal schedule was abandoned. Emily gathered with a group of girls at an upstairs window that commanded a good view of the Amherst road. The weather was miserable. Harsh winds drove sheets of cold rain against the glass. Mt. Holyoke, which usually dominated the perspective to the north, was completely obscured. It was difficult even to identify carriages that paused at the seminary. Looking down from above, the patient watchers saw the exodus for vacation as a pageant of scurrying black umbrella tops.

Hour after hour passed and no one came for the two Emilys. No morning in her life had ever passed so slowly for Emily Dickinson. Emily Norcross by now shared a good measure of her excitement and looked for Austin as anxiously as her cousin. It must have been the thousandth time that Emily Dickinson peered through the rain for her tardy brother when, wonder of wonders, she spied the family carriage approaching.

With a shriek she ran to her room, collected her belongings, and when Austin's arrival was announced, raced downstairs with an abandon that almost bowled her tall, dignified-looking brother off his feet.

In no time they were all three in the carriage and heading north. The rain and wind lashed their vehicle without mercy as it jolted along the streaming mountain road. Despite the weather their progress was rapid enough to satisfy Emily. Eventually the Amherst College buildings and the spire of First Church loomed through the grayness. At the door of the Dickinsons' big white house waited her pleased father, her beaming sister, Mother with tears in her eyes, and even an hospitable-looking pussy. Emily at last was home, and she was overjoyed.

Four days passed swiftly, filled with events familiar and beloved by Emily. On Thanksgiving morning the family attended church to hear a good sermon from their own Reverend Mr. Colton. After the traditional, bountiful Thanksgiving dinner, Emily, Vinnie, and cousin Emily made calls on friends. Four invitations for that evening necessitated declining two. The whole Dickinson family chose to spend a happy hour with a group gathered at the home of Amherst College rhetoric professor Aaron Warner. Then the young people went on to Mrs. Samuel Mack's, where other friends were gaily engaged in playing games and having a candy scrape. At ten o'clock the young Dickinsons returned home, Austin carrying a gleaming lantern to light the way. Father was waiting up. He hoped Emily would play him a few tunes on the piano. Emily obliged by both playing and singing, then the whole family retired.

Monday morning found a forlorn Emily Dickinson back within the cheerless walls of Mount Holyoke Seminary. She was now, at sixteen, the youngest member of the middle class and was about to plunge into studying chemistry, physiology, Euclid, and algebra. She could look to no more holidays until the term ended in late January. Orthodox Congregational communities like Amherst and South Hadley did not make a celebration of Christmas.

As Mount Holyoke's curriculum unfolded to Emily Dickinson, another aspect of the school's life also began to grow in momentum. The seminary had been founded for the purpose of educating young women to teach, but Mary Lyon was as concerned with the religious condition of her students as with their academic achievement. "Never engage to teach where you cannot give religious instruction" was one of her dictums. At the seminary she conducted a strenuous program of devotions and prayer meetings in the attempt to bring her young ladies into the Christian fold. Imbued with her spirit of Christian endeavor, many of her teachers and students went on to become missionaries.

Early in each academic year it was Miss Lyon's habit to call a meeting of the whole school. At the meeting the seminary students were divided into two groups, those who felt an awareness of God's presence in their lives and thus "indulged a hope" of being a Christian, and those who did not. No person was a Christian simply by birthright. It was a condition arrived at through constant striving and, finally, some inner personal knowledge of God's grace. Mary Lyon saw it her duty to bring as many of her students as she could to this happy state. Those who desired to reach it but had not were called impenitent.

At the first important religious gathering of the school, Miss Lyon asked those who indulged a hope to stand. Their names were taken. Then those without hope were asked to rise. It was a solemn occasion, often bringing tears to the eyes of girls who could not conscientiously say they had found God. In the fall of 1847 Emily Dickinson's name was put on the list of those who had no hope.

Mary Lyon met for morning devotions with her students in the big seminary hall on the main floor. She read from the Bible, then spoke at length upon such themes as man's relationship to God or human sin or eternity. In the afternoon she again gathered her students together, this time for advice of a more practical nature. The need to stay in good health or the sinfulness of wasting time reading light books were typical topics. Through all she said shone Mary Lyon's great religious fervor.

As the weeks went by Miss Lyon called prayer meetings for the two groups into which the school was spiritually divided. She extended invitations for inquirers to begin seeking the salvation of their souls. It was her hope to swell the ranks of Christians as the year progressed. Since the founding of the school, revivals had occurred regularly among the students. The year before Emily entered, the revival had been a powerful one. By the end of the final term all but 20 of the 185 students professed themselves Christians. Mary Lyon dared not hope for evidence of God's presence again so soon, yet she worked quietly and diligently with her impenitent girls in hope of some response.

During the second term a perceptible stir in religious interest took place. While lessons and recitations went on as usual, there was a growing solemnity among the young ladies. Mary Lyon held prayer meetings for those without hope with increasing frequency.

For the second time in her life Emily felt the strong urge to join those who were giving up their hearts to Christ. Her experience of two winters before, however, made her wary. Then she had quickly succumbed to an emotional urgency and just as quickly lost interest. This time she was determined to follow a more rational course.

The religious atmosphere of the school grew more and more intense as December went on. Emily Norcross was very deeply affected. Near Christmas she joined the group of girls who indulged hope. Emily Dickinson rejoiced for her. From Christmas on she knew the prayers of her roommate often concerned her own hardness of heart, for with twenty-four others in the middle class Emily Dickinson was still without hope.

The day before Christmas was set aside as a fast day.

Nearly all observed it. A few evenings later Mary Lyon invited those who "wanted religion" to meet with her in Room B. Emily Dickinson left her books to slip into the crowded classroom. The evening's session took the form of a series of questions. Did the gathered impenitents feel they were willing to give up the world? Miss Lyon asked. Were they ready to bow their will to God, to see their portion in Him? After readings from the Bible and prayers, the school's preceptress requested those who wanted this day to be entirely employed in the service of Christ to stand. Emily felt she could not conscientiously rise. The girls around her stood, one by one, until all in the room were on their feet except Emily. There she sat, small and rigid and solemn-eyed, looking straight ahead. It was a very conspicuous thing for her to do. She was far from unconcerned with her religious condition, yet she appeared the opposite to the eyes in that hushed room.

In later times Emily explained the matter quite simply to a friend. "They thought it queer I didn't rise," she said. "I thought a lie would be queerer." It was a small incident, misunderstood, but, as is frequently the way, it was whispered around the school, from student to student and teacher to teacher. From that time on all kept an eye upon her progress in becoming a Christian.

Emily kept the turmoil bottled up inside her. She made no mention of it in letters home, but she was feeling its strain. She was studying very hard and also enduring constant anxiety. She grew pale and thin, and the ever-present tide of homesickness took advantage of her frequently during these cold, dreary winter weeks. Yet she made the effort to write cheerfully to Austin, whose imaginative letters kept her spirits from flagging completely. On January 17 of the new year she confided to Abiah, "There is a great deal of religious interest here and many are flocking to the ark of safety. I have not yet given up to the claims of Christ, but trust I am not entirely thoughtless on so important & serious a subject." That evening she was one of seventeen girls who attended Miss Lyon's meeting for those who felt "an uncommon anxiety to decide."

Four days later the term ended. Edward Dickinson must have been surprised to see how thin and tired his daughter looked when she stepped from the sleigh to her own doorstep. He asked no questions, requested no explanations; but when the two-week vacation was over it had been decided that once Emily completed the current school year she would not return to Mount Holyoke Seminary.

By the time the third term started in February, the religious spell had been broken for Emily. She did not again work up to such a pitch about becoming a Christian, but neither did she dismiss the subject from her mind, nor cease entirely to attend prayer meetings for the impenitent. She remained far from happy about her undetermined state.

One of the bright spots in a long, monotonous winter was the occurrence of Valentine Week. Instead of valentine-sending being reserved for a single day, clever notes and witty verses flew among young people throughout the entire week. Valentines were the perfect outlet for Emily Dickinson's originality and her flair for high foolishness. She usually sent several poems or mock-serious essays to particular friends, each valentine as close to a masterpiece of wit as she could make it.

But Mary Lyon frowned on valentines. She thought them foolish and forbade her students to send them. Some of the girls, having foreknowledge of Miss Lyon's sentiments, made advance arrangements with the South Hadley post-master for posting their valentines at the appropriate time. When Miss Lyon's assistant, Miss Whitman, caught wind of the plot, she stormed to the post office, hoping to catch the contraband valentines and learn the names of the disobedient young ladies. But the postmaster, known as "a good hand to help the girls," managed to frustrate Miss Whitman's attack entirely.

For the first time in years Emily Dickinson neither sent nor received any valentines. She commented wistfully to Austin that "Probably, Mary, Abby & Viny have received scores of them from the infatuated wights in the neighborhood while your *highly accomplished & gifted elder sister* is entirely overlooked."

In mid-March the seminary's long-dreaded semiannual oral examinations took place. For five days the teachers interrogated their students on all the subjects they had studied for two and a half terms. The examinations were open to the public, and announcements appeared in local newspapers inviting all who might be interested to attend. Emily Dickinson, who always dreaded tests of her knowledge, and dreaded even more being examined before a roomful of strangers, was undoubtedly delighted that bad weather kept people away every day but the last.

The week before examinations found her reviewing feverishly. She sat in her little room before a table stacked with books and notebooks and scattered with several handkerchiefs. Despite the diligence with which she and Emily Norcross stoked the fire in their fireplace, she had caught a bad cold in the end-of-winter chill that penetrated the seminary building. Instead of improving, she got steadily worse.

During the week after examinations a friend from Amherst, possibly Abby Wood, came to stay with Emily at the seminary. That friend bore home to Mr. and Mrs. Dickinson the details of Emily's poor health. Immediately the long, strong arm of Edward Dickinson reached across the Holyoke Mountains, plucked Emily out of school, and brought her home to bed.

Tears and protests were of no avail. Emily kept up her

studies at home, but was not permitted by her father to return to school until the beginning of spring term, a month and a half later. "Father is quite a hand to give medicine," reported Emily, "especially if it is not desirable to the patient, and I was dosed for about a month after my return home, without any mercy, till at last out of mere pity my cough went away, and I had quite a season of peace."

While at home Emily made a new friend. Benjamin Franklin Newton was a young man who had begun studying law in Edward Dickinson's office. Emily discovered that his literary education was far broader than hers, discouraged as she had been by her father from indulging in popular novels or books containing liberal ideas. Now, at Ben Newton's direction, she had a "feast in the reading line." She devoured Longfellow's *Evangeline* and Tennyson's *The Princess,* and also sampled several novels before returning to school.

By mid-May spring had come to New England. The brown landscape turned green and yellow. Wildflowers in field and wood tempted young people to find their hiding places. "The older I grow, the more do I love spring and spring flowers," exclaimed Emily, having already searched out the trailing arbutus, yellow violet, bloodroot, and adder's tongue. So diligent had been the picking of eleven generations of seminary students that Miss Lyon was forced to restrict the ardor of those pupils studying botany for fear that certain species would soon be extinct around South Hadley.

As the weather grew increasingly delightful, and as the end of her time at boarding school drew near, Emily's spirits rose. The burden of homesickness she continually bore lightened, and her last days at the seminary were contentedly dedicated to hard study indoors and pleasant wanderings through summer fields and country lanes out-doors.

In early August the Holyoke Anniversary, or graduation exercises, was held. After it was over, Emily, for the last time and with no regrets, rode northward over the Holyoke Mountains, through the Notch, to Amherst. She knew her father intended to keep her home a year, after which he might send her somewhere else for further study. Until now her life had followed a well-defined path; the way ahead appeared uncertain.

Four

Excitement charged the air from the very start. To begin, the back-yard cherry tree set a tone of gaiety by providing its first fruits for the tea table.

Then Mrs. Dickinson took out her beautiful new bonnet, bought and sent from Boston by Austin, who was there teaching school.

When Emily and Vinnie had donned their gloves and bonnets and, despite the warm July weather, their best merino shawls, the Dickinsons were ready to leave the house.

At precisely six o'clock Squire Dickinson, his glossy

beaver hat tall upon his head, assisted his wife and two daughters into the public stage for the hour's drive to Northampton. Although the performance at the First Congregational Church did not begin until eight o'clock, they were determined to be in good time to hear the famous Swedish Nightingale, Jenny Lind, who was charming northeastern America with her golden voice this summer of 1851.

It was well they started early. Hardly had the stage commenced its journey when it began lurching and jolting violently. For a few desperate moments the Dickinson ladies clung in terror to the hand straps, to their bonnets, and to each other. Then the mad motion ceased and they climbed out. One of the horses had tried to bolt. It stood wild-eyed in the traces, refusing now to budge another step.

When the driver had procured another horse, Edward Dickinson helped his shaken family back into the coach. This time they proceeded with no more than normal joggling over the dirt highway to Northampton. Past thick green woods and marshes profuse with flowering weeds they rolled, chatting of the performance to come and of Austin's recent comments about the celebrated Jenny. Austin had heard her sing in Boston the preceding week, and, unlike almost everyone else, had not been overwhelmed. It tickled Edward Dickinson that his son dissented from the mounting acclaim for the singer. Had Austin's letter arrived a day earlier, the Squire declared, it would have seen publication in Amherst's weekly newspaper.

A sudden peal of thunder, audibly different from the steady rumbling of the carriage wheels, set four faces looking anxiously upward from the stage windows. The sky ahead was rapidly filling with ominous black clouds which cut the evening light to quick dusk. Edward Dickinson consulted his pocket watch.

"I doubt we'll beat a rainstorm," he informed his family. Almost as he spoke, gusts of wind rocked the stage. Trees along the road bowed and shook and showed the pale green undersides of their leaves in warning of approaching storm. A few fat drops fell. Then the rain pelted in earnest. Within minutes a drenching torrent of water poured down on the stage, obliterating the view to either side. The horses slowed, but plodded on through the heavy downpour. Licks of lightning and claps of thunder accompanied the stage across the Connecticut River bridge into Northampton.

Despite the weather, the First Congregational Church was filled to overflowing by eight o'clock. Dark-coated gentlemen and ladies in damp finery excitedly anticipated the rare entertainment. It began with short recitals by local talent. Then came Jenny. Like a child she appeared, small and fair and simply dressed, with blue eyes filled with longing. She sang "I know that my Redeemer Liveth" and

"Home Sweet Home," and her listeners applauded madly. Bouquets were brought forward. Cries of "encore" swept the audience. Jenny obliged with the "Bird Song," a wild melody full of bird-like sounds and trills. Emily Dickinson, clapping enthusiastically, glanced sideways at her father. On his face was an expression Emily had never seen before. Was it anger? Silliness? Embarrassment? Emily couldn't describe it. "It was'nt *sarcasm* exactly, nor it was'nt *disdain,* it was infinitely funnier than either of those virtues," Emily later wrote Austin, "as if old Abraham had come to see the show, and thought it all very well, but a little excess of *Monkey!*"

"Good evening, sir," said Squire Dickinson when the performers bowed. "Very well—that will do," when they retired. To Emily he was a performance in himself.

Jenny sang "Comin' Through the Rye" and other melodies, all enthusiastically acclaimed by the crowd packed into the pews. "How we all loved Jennie Lind, but not accustomed oft to her manner of singing, did'nt fancy *that* so well as we did *her,*" remarked the observant Emily. At last the Swedish Nightingale ceased singing and was whisked away from Northampton by train. The great event was over.

Sometime after midnight the Dickinsons were delivered safely to their front door. Wearily they bade each other good-night, and even Emily, whose habit it had become to work at her writing stand before retiring, went straight to bed.

Emily was twenty years old now, a diminutive girl, not over five feet two inches tall. Still plain, her chief beauty was her lovely auburn hair, which she wore parted in the middle and pulled straight back into a net behind her head. Her dark eyes, which she described as the color of sherry left in a glass, were remarkably close to her hair in hue.

She was not pretty, as Vinnie was, but she did not lack callers. Students and tutors from the college, friends of Austin's, cousins, young men from Father's law office, all rang the Dickinsons' doorbell to visit with both girls and invite them buggy-riding over country roads.

Vinnie they sought for her coquettish airs, Emily more for her sprightly mind. She was shy, painfully so at times. There were social situations she would go to extremes to avoid. But once a friendship was established her sensitivity was sheathed in warmth and wit, and she made a delightful companion.

Emily's friendship with Ben Newton, the young law student in Father's office, had blossomed quickly the year following her return from Mount Holyoke. Ben was almost ten years older than she and of a more liberal cast of mind than any person Emily had had opportunity to know. She soon became his eager pupil, following the guidance of his well-defined literary tastes to a wealth of new books and ideas. Father could scarcely be expected to approve his daughter's new literary diet. He himself read only "lonely and rigorous" books. "Modern Literati," he scornfully termed such currently popular authors as Charles Dickens and Harriet Beecher Stowe, author of *Uncle Tom's Cabin*.

Ben Newton introduced Emily to the writings of the Brontës and the liberal books of Lydia Maria Child, a feminist and early advocate of abolishing slavery. Ben admired Ralph Waldo Emerson long before that writer had won his reputation as New England's sage. He gave Emily an early copy of Emerson's poems. Now nearly thirty, Ben had had cause to formulate his religious convictions. He could discuss with Emily many of the questions that deeply puzzled her about God and immortality.

Ben found Emily an ideal scholar. She read the books he brought her, seized the core of their ideas, and confronted him with penetrating questions and speculations. Their discussions ranged from politics to poetry. Emily had tried writing some verses. She showed them to Ben, who praised them and encouraged her to write better ones. Someday, he told her, she might be a poet. Emily hugged the idea close to her as a golden dream, and at night worked at her writing table to make it come true.

Ben didn't stay in Amherst. Late in the summer of 1849 he returned to his home in Worcester to enter law practice.

In Emily's autograph album he left the cryptic message, "All can write autographs, but few paragraphs, for we are mostly no more than *names*."

Emily missed her preceptor, as she called him, more than she could admit to anyone. They began a correspondence which kept up even after Ben chose a wife and married in 1851. His encouragement of her literary efforts came now by mail, but his enthusiasm did not fail her.

Life was far from dull for Emily despite Ben's going, for she was caught up in the modest social life of the small but dignified New England town. Young men and women her age took pleasure in sleigh rides, maple sugar parties, Shakespeare reading clubs, candy scrapes, and evenings of charades. Gentlemen and young ladies paid calls on one another, took walks, and, when a horse and carriage was available, went riding. Popular excursions among groups of young people included picnics at Orient Springs in the Pelham Hills and trips to the hotel atop Mount Holyoke. The view of the Connecticut Valley from the summit of Mount Holyoke was spectacular, thought unequaled even by many who had traveled extensively in Europe. One reached the hotel either by climbing the steep pitch on foot, no small accomplishment for long-skirted ladies, or by riding its famed cog railway. The railway was an open car pulled by horsepowered pulley up wooden tracks at an angle that defied gravity. A third choice was to climb the eight-hundred-odd wooden steps running alongside the railway.

One clear, bright October day Emily and Vinnie, together with the Haskell sisters and three male escorts, climbed to the mountain house. There they gratefully sipped cold lemonade and registered in the guest book. Emily looked down on the Connecticut River coiling lazily through a patchwork of green and brown fields, crimson and yellow woods. Shifting her gaze she could see mountains sixty miles away on the distant horizon. It was a breathtaking sight. She must have felt she lived in the most beautiful spot on earth.

Emily was twenty. Her formal education was at an end. Until such time as she might marry and move away, she was expected to live with her parents in that nebulous state known as "at home." Household duties occupied some of her time. What she termed "the path of duty" occupied another small part, although Emily rebelled against paying calls on Amherst's sick and aged, and refused to sew for the poor with the church ladies. She found greater pleasure in reading and tending her flowers.

Her friends occupied her, and the small circle who made up her intimates was very dear to her. She spent hours walking and talking with Jane Humphrey and Emily Fowler, Sue Gilbert and her sister Mattie. Sentimentality was much in vogue among young ladies. Emily Dickinson indulged as freely as any other girl in twining arms, sweet sighs, and soulful confidences. When any of her friends were away from Amherst Emily wrote long mournful letters protesting her devotion and her need for reciprocating love.

Among her male friends had been Leonard Humphrey, who was principal at the academy for several years. His sudden death in 1850 moved Emily and many others in Amherst very deeply. George Gould, a classmate of Austin's, was another good friend. Intelligent and clever, George was editor of the college newspaper. Emily attended many lectures and social functions with him until he graduated. Their common love of drollery reached its zenith one Valentine Week when Emily composed a long letter that began, "Magnum bonum, 'harum scarum,' zounds et zounds, et war alarum . . ." George turned the tables by promptly publishing it in his newspaper.

During 1850 Father had sent Vinnie away for two terms at Ipswich Female Seminary. Emily missed her sister terribly, missed her funny remarks and those "perpendicular times" when Vinnie sent a roomful of young people into screaming laughter with her imitation of a particular Amherst matron advancing up the street to meeting. Almost as funny to Emily was the sight of Vinnie moved to tears by her own soulful piano rendition of a popular song called "Are We Almost There?"

While at Ipswich Vinnie came under the spell of a

revival. She wrote to Austin pleading that he give himself to Christ and hoping that he and Emily might join her in becoming Christian. Amherst was likewise undergoing a powerful revival, both at the college and in town. Once again Emily witnessed the solemn change occurring in her friends. Abby Wood, Mary Warner, Jane Humphrey, and Sue Gilbert all heeded the call of Christ, while Emily had to report once more, "I am one of the lingering *bad* ones, and so do I slink away, and pause, and ponder, and ponder, and pause, and do work without knowing why—not surely for *this* brief world, and more sure it is not for Heaven— and I ask what this message *means* that they ask for so very eagerly. . . ."

If Emily did not know, her father at last decided he did. It was rumored that the Reverend Mr. Colton had had to admonish Edward Dickinson about trying to come to Christ as a lawyer rather than as a poor sinner, and had advised him to get down and pray for his condition. Whatever the route, the Squire was one of seventy persons who joined the Church by profession of faith one August Sabbath morning.

Edward Dickinson was Amherst's leading lawyer and a busy man. Scarcely an issue of the local paper appeared without mentioning his name in connection with some civic or legal affair. He was the moving force that brought the railroad to Amherst. He firmly believed the railroad was the greatest thing that had happened to Amherst since the founding of the college. The selling of the last share of stock in the Amherst-Belchertown line was the signal for actual construction to begin, and Amherst celebrated the occasion with a great bonfire. Father was "realy *sober* from excessive satisfaction," reported Emily.

Another bonfire in December, 1852, celebrated the election of the Honorable Edward Dickinson to the House of Representatives in Washington. It was a great day for Amherst and for the local Whig party. The bonfire burned late into the night.

Next morning a small boy met Squire Dickinson walking sedately down North Pleasant Street to his office.

"Fine bonfire we had, sir," the youth presumed.

"Yes," answered Edward Dickinson drily, "I noticed my woodpile had grown smaller during the night."

Duties occasionally took the Squire away from Amherst for days at a time. Even when he was at home he spent many evenings out of the house caring for civic concerns. If friends came calling on Lavinia and Emily during Father's absence, they would enjoy an hour or two of conversation, perhaps interspersed with melodies on the piano by one of the girls. Emily was an excellent pianist. She still studied music seriously and created her own improvisations. Vinnie was less serious about music, prone to learn the latest pieces, which she often accompanied with her own singing. But evenings when Father was at home, and he and youthful callers collided, were dreadful.

One winter evening in 1852 as Emily and Vinnie were helping their mother clear the table after tea, the front door bell rang loudly.

Vinnie answered, and shortly returned to the kitchen to announce that Brainerd Harrington, an Amherst College senior and friend of Austin's, wanted to see Emily.

The usual wave of shyness stole over Emily as she went timidly to meet Brainerd. When she passed the sitting room a loud command issued from Father, who was in his armchair before the fire recovering from an attack of rheumatism.

"Don't stand at the door, Emily!"

Not stand at the door! What should she do then, Emily wondered wildly? Surely she wasn't going to ask Mr. Harrington in and try to entertain him in front of Father! In desperation she closed the hall door, shutting herself into the cold entry with Brainerd. At least it kept the draft off Father.

To her relief, Brainerd decided not to stay. He had another errand to perform and knew the Squire wasn't well. Having delivered his message to Emily, he left quickly.

Emily fled past the parlor back to the kitchen, where she found her mother and Vinnie shaking with laughter. They made Emily cross, but before she could remonstrate, the door bell rang a second time.

Vinnie opened the front door to William Cowper Dickinson, a distant cousin, now a tutor at the college. He was a welcome guest in the Dickinson household, which this winter sorely missed the absent Austin. Willie had brought news interesting to Father, so he settled in the sitting room. When the bell rang once again to announce the arrival of Ben Thurston, an Amherst senior who was bent on seeing the Dickinson girls, Emily was forced to join the party. She sank with dread upon the sofa and endeavored to make general conversation before her frozen-faced, rheumatic sire.

"It was amazingly cold today, for March," ventured Emily.

"It was," agreed Mr. Thurston. Vinnie and Willie nodded in assent. Father cleared his throat.

Never, thought Emily, had she witnessed such wonderful unanimity. It was followed by utter silence.

Let's see, Emily thought frantically, crossing off in her mind categories she knew better than to discuss in front of her father. Not books, not music, and, please Lord, not the railroad.

"Didn't the Reverend Mr. Bliss preach remarkably on Sunday?" she suggested with sudden inspiration.

Again the company, sitting uncomfortably forward in their chairs, agreed.

"He's quite a remarkable man, really, don't you think?" Emily rattled on, addressing herself to Ben Thurston, who looked as if he had recently gagged. "I felt much of his forcefulness can be attributed to his having such a majestic head. His eyes, you know, with such fierce brows." Emily felt the absurdity of what she was saying bubbling up inside her. With her next remark the absurdity boiled over.

"He seems to me to quite resemble the Reverend George Whitefield, don't you think?"

Edward Dickinson shot such a baleful look at his daughter that Emily twitched. Mr. Whitefield had been dead almost a century. Emily had never so much as seen his ashes, as Edward Dickinson was well aware.

Luckily she was saved by the unexpected arrival of cousin Thankful Smith, who had driven from Hadley to see Mr. and Mrs. Dickinson. Father decided to entertain his generation by the kitchen fire, and left the young people to themselves. Willie and Ben and Emily and Vinnie enjoyed the rest of the evening thoroughly.

Times with Father were frequently gloomy, especially with Austin away. "We don't *have* many jokes tho' *now*, it is pretty much all sobriety, and we do not have much poetry, father having made up his mind that its pretty much all *real life*," complained Emily to her brother.

But occasionally Father surprised his family enough to set them wondering if they would ever truly understand him. Shortly after the sun had set one clear, crisp fall evening, the whole town was startled by the sudden loud clanging of a church bell. Rushing into the street in the expectation of a disastrous fire, Amherst citizens beheld a crimson sky in which gold-pink rays shot from a center brilliance—no fire, but a magnificent display of northern lights which lasted fully fifteen minutes. And the person who had rung the church bell to bring this glory of nature to the attention of the townspeople was none other than Edward Dickinson.

If the Dickinson children were finding it a strain to get along with Father, the Squire in turn was having problems handling his offspring.

Lavinia was seeing a lot of the young tutor William Howland, who in his spare time from Amherst College was studying law in Edward Dickinson's office. Mr. Dickinson liked Howland very much, but he was far from pleased to return unexpectedly early from a Springfield business trip one day and find Vinnie paying Howland a visit at the law office at a time she knew her father to be away. Mr. and Mrs. Dickinson were even more displeased when Vinnie rode off to Ware with Howland for an entire day when she distinctly knew her parents objected to the excursion. Lavinia was becoming a shade too disrespectful for her father's pleasure.

Emily, too, had a fair supply of admirers, although the

only one Edward Dickinson seriously objected to was that classmate of Austin's, George Gould, who fortunately had left Amherst after his commencement. Admittedly he was bright, but he was also poor as a church mouse and planning to go into the ministry. He would never earn enough to care for Emily properly.

Other things about Emily disturbed the Squire. His elder daughter was cleverer than his younger about doing as she liked. She made no scenes. She simply went her own way. Take the church problem, for instance. Emily occasionally rebelled against going to meeting. Should the weather prove raw, Emily would beg off accompanying the family to First Church by making gentle references to her slender constitution. Emily *was* susceptible to chest colds and she *did* become fatigued easily, but sometimes Edward Dickinson almost suspected she rejoiced in inclement Sabbaths.

This queer shyness of Emily's, too, was becoming worse instead of better. She wouldn't answer the door if there was anyone else to do it. Sometimes she would fly upstairs to avoid conversing with visitors. You never could tell if she was going to attend lyceum lectures or her reading club. She seemed completely capricious.

If Austin were home, perhaps things would be different. The girls adored him. He could make them listen to reason. But Austin had been away teaching school in Boston and now was attending Harvard Law School. Edward Dickinson missed the son in whom he took such pride. It was true that on the rare occasions when Austin could get home, they seemed at swords' points a good part of the time, but when Austin was away, his father could hardly wait to hear from him. Emily reported to Austin:

"He reads all the letters you write as soon as he gets, at the post office, no matter to whom addressed . . . then he makes me read them loud at the supper table again, and when he gets home in the evening, he cracks a few walnuts, puts his spectacles on, and with your last in hand, sits down to enjoy the evening. He remarked in confidence to me this morning, that he 'guessed you saw through things there'—of course I answered 'yes sir,' but what the thought conveyed I remained in happy ignorance. Whether he meant to say that you saw through *the Judges,* overcoats and all, I could not quite determine but I'm sure he designed to compliment you very highly."

Her brother's absence caused a great gap in Emily's life, for Austin was a source of fun and excitement. His presence created a stir that all the members of the family missed, and that was recaptured only briefly in the funny letters he sent home.

Emily wrote to Austin regularly, usually every Sunday. She missed her early-morning confidant, for whenever Austin was home he would join her downstairs before the others were up. While Emily heated the meat and potatoes and brown bread and made the tea for breakfast, the two shared many opinions and secrets.

Emily's letters were extraordinary, agreed all who read them. She didn't fill them with mere facts, but sent her thoughts. Vinnie accused her sister of feeding Austin on air, and frequently enclosed a note in the same envelope telling Austin the latest births and deaths, the comings and goings of friends and relatives.

Knowing that Austin was lonely and did enjoy bits of information about home-life, Emily made a greater effort to include practical details in letters to him than in letters to other friends. But with her skill in writing increasing, she could not resist trying out her literary abilities, too. She was still secretly writing poems, and sending the best of them to Ben Newton. Only last week she had had an especially encouraging letter from Ben. He had ended by an oddly worded promise to pay her a visit when she had achieved her goal of becoming a poet. "If I live, I will go to Amherst," he had written. "If I die, I certainly will."

Emily sat at the kitchen table on an end-of-March morning in 1853 writing to her brother. Austin had sent verses of his own in his last letter. He was obviously quite proud of them. Emily found them overly soulful, but beyond that she was determined Austin should not gain too inflated an opinion of his own talents. She took up her pen;

cocked her head to one side, and delivered herself of some roguish remarks:

"And Austin is a Poet, Austin writes a psalm. Out of the way, Pegasus, Olympus enough 'to him,' and just say to those 'nine muses' that we have done with them! . . .

"Now Brother Pegasus, I'll tell you what it is—I've been in the habit *myself* of writing some few things, and it rather appears to me that you're getting away my patent, so you'd better be somewhat careful, or I'll call the police!"

Emily wrote gaily on, finally ending with love from all the family. She set the letter aside and found a paring knife to help her mother peel apples for a pie. Mrs. Dickinson was an excellent cook and Emily her apt pupil, for of all household duties Emily far and away preferred cooking. The warm kitchen, the lovely smells, the savory dishes created from minced this and sifted that, appealed to her far more than dusting and mopping and beating. She could not abide cleaning; she preferred pestilence. Luckily Vinnie was agreeable to helping with that part of the housework, letting Emily share the cooking. Whenever Mother and Vinnie covered their heads with cheesecloth, rolled up their sleeves, and began tugging the carpets this way and that, Emily would flee to her room in consternation and lock her door. The whole experience truly upset her.

Toward noon Vinnie, who had been doing errands at

Kellogg's General Store, brought in some bundles and the day's mail. The two family cats hopped down off sunny window sills to greet their favorite mistress. Emily found no letters addressed to her. She took up the daily *Springfield Republican* and settled herself upon the kitchen stool to scan its pages. She glanced briefly at the obituaries, and suddenly let a small cry escape.

Lavinia and Mother flew to her side. Emily, nearly stunned, pointed to two short lines that announced the death of Benjamin Franklin Newton.

Emily's world spun. Ben had always been reticent about the ill health that had long plagued him. Now he was dead of consumption. "If I live, I will go to Amherst. If I die, I certainly will." Suddenly she understood what Ben had meant. It was a gentle warning of his approaching death. Sometime later Emily picked up her pen and added on the envelope flap of the letter to Austin: "Monday noon. Oh Austin, Newton is dead. The first of my own friends. Pace."

Emily was not unacquainted with death. No one living during the nineteenth century could be, for medical knowledge was limited and childbirth, incurable disease, and epidemics carried people away with regular frequency. At least one friend had died during Emily's childhood, and the deaths of Leonard Humphrey and, more recently, Emily Norcross of Monson touched her closely. But none of these pierced her heart and soul as did the death of Ben Newton, whom Emily Dickinson later called the friend who taught her immortality but himself ventured too near.

Ben's going affected her life in a way that was barely perceptible at first. Underneath her sadness her mind churned with questions his death raised about life and death and the world to come. Where was Ben now? He had possessed a faith in an unseen world. Was he with God?

Still deeply disturbed many months later, Emily wrote to Ben Newton's minister in Worcester. She apologized for intruding but needed to know more about Ben's attitude of mind as he approached death. Had he been "willing" to die? Congregational Church doctrine preached that one did not otherwise reach the Kingdom of Heaven.

Only after he was irretrievably gone did Emily begin to estimate Ben's worth and the valuable contribution he had made to her own intellectual growth. She worked doggedly on at her writing with only her lexicon now for companionship. Her true inspiration was dead. Long years later Emily wrote a poem in tribute to Ben Newton, calling him at the conclusion·

> . . . *the Pearl—*
> *That slipped my simple fingers through—*
> *While just a Girl at School.*

His death marked the beginning of her maturity. It was a painful beginning. Emily wrote wistfully to Austin, "I wish we were *always* children, how to grow up I dont know."

Austin, however, was approaching adult life with less hesitancy than his sister. He had long been interested in his sisters' good friends Sue and Mattie Gilbert. Now he discovered that he and Sue were falling in love. Their match evolved slowly and secretly during the period Austin was attending law school. The courtship had the ups and downs common to a union of two independent, strong-willed persons. Sue was noted for her striking good looks and her cleverness. Emily and Vinnie loved her; Edward Dickinson had long admired her; the forthcoming marriage promised to be a happy event.

A young man poised to launch his career and marriage in mid-nineteenth–century America could not fail to be alert to the greatest dynamic force of his time: the building of the West. The population was expanding rapidly westward, changing frontier country to fast-growing towns and cities. Opportunities for men of enthusiasm, intelligence, and initiative seemed boundless. Austin Dickinson graduated from law school in 1854 determined to marry Sue and enter law practice in a growing, energetic western community, hopefully Chicago. Father had other ideas.

Amherst had provided ample exercise for the energies and talents of Edward Dickinson. He was certain his son could make a challenging career of helping the town keep

pace with the growth of the rest of the country. Currently
in the midst of serving his congressional term in Washington, Squire Dickinson had a sense of the national pulse and
he anticipated that New England would play a mighty
role in the country's expansion and development. Basically,
too, his fierce love and unexpressed need for his children
made the thought of parting with any of them unbearable.
During the spring of 1855 the Squire bought back the old
Dickinson homestead on Main Street. He offered to build
his son a brand new house next door and to take him as full
partner into his law firm if Austin would only stay in Amherst. After due consideration, and with admitted sacrifice
of spirit, Austin agreed.

During Edward Dickinson's second winter in Congress
his two daughters visited him in Washington. The Squire
hoped the journey would have a beneficial effect on Emily,
who had been causing him considerable uneasiness of late.
She seemed to be afflicted by a lingering spell of melancholia, or at least what the Squire called melancholia for
lack of another name. During the past year or more she had
become rather retiring in her ways, spending most of her
time at home, being extremely selective about whom she
saw and where she went. Her father was sure there was
something on her mind, but she did not talk to him about
it and he would not probe. She welcomed privacy, whether
in her bedroom or on solitary walks in the woods and

meadows. To soothe certain parental anxieties about the latter habit, the Squire bought her a large brown dog. Emily named him Carlo, and readily accepted her "shaggy ally."

Emily was aware of her father's concern, although she sensed too that her preference for home and her willingness to provide little attentions for her father were far from displeasing to him. Her preoccupation was with her spiritual condition. She was still at the mercy of doubts and questions that had assailed her since Ben's death. Like any New Englander conscientiously brought up in an orthodox Congregational Church, Emily knew it was high time for her to determine her religious convictions. Others of her friends had done so. Vinnie had joined the Church by confession of faith; Austin was about to. Sue Gilbert had pushed Emily almost beyond the limits of friendship about becoming a Church member.

But Emily had inherited her father's puritanical honesty, which, in combination with her deeply inquiring nature, kept her examining what was written and what she knew of life, death, and God's relationship to man to try to get at the truth. To join the Church she would have to accept certain dogmas and biblical interpretations the Congregational Church held as true. Some of them, however, held no meaning for Emily Dickinson, and she would not compromise her honesty to accept them, not "on faith" or any other grounds. She preferred to remain outside the Church.

In an age when religious conviction was a very serious concern among young people, Emily alienated some of her Amherst friends by her unconventional attitude. Sensitive to their criticism, Emily began spending her time with the few who understood her. Meanwhile, if the Church did not provide a satisfactory solution to her quest for spiritual knowledge, she would look in other directions as well. She found insight in some of the books her father bought her (but begged her not to read) and in the minds of a few people she met.

On the trip to Washington she met many interesting people. She enjoyed the new sights, the dinner parties, a visit to George Washington's beautiful Mount Vernon. Back to Amherst went the story that at dinner one evening Emily had delighted an elderly chief justice by asking, as a flaming plum pudding was brought on, "Oh, Sir, may one eat of hell-fire with impunity here?" Emily was gayer and less shy than she had been for a long time.

Journeying home, Vinnie and Emily stopped in Philadelphia to visit an old friend, Eliza Coleman, who had lived in Amherst and attended the academy with both girls. On Sabbath morning the Colemans took the Dickinson girls to the Arch Street Presbyterian Church to hear the Reverend Charles Wadsworth, one of the most popular preachers of the day. It was an experience Emily never forgot.

Charles Wadsworth was about forty years old and he was far from handsome. Yet the overwhelming power of his oratory and the obvious depth of his conviction convinced Emily he might provide her the spiritual guidance she sought. Eventually, after her return to Amherst, she wrote to Mr. Wadsworth seeking his help in reconciling the Church's teachings with her own religious convictions.

> *Experiment to me*
> *Is every one I meet*
> *If it contain a Kernel?*
> *The Figure of a Nut*
>
> *Presents upon a Tree*
> *Equally plausibly,*
> *But Meat within, is requisite*
> *To Squirrels and to Me.*

Emily wrote this poem during her thirties, but she lived its philosophy while in her twenties and to some extent had always lived it. She had begun losing touch with early friends like Abiah Root, with whom she no longer had much in common. She found a few new friends who possessed the requisite "meat within." One was her cousin John Graves. Another was tiny, warmly humorous Elizabeth Holland, wife of Dr. Josiah Holland of Springfield, the

assistant editor of the *Springfield Republican*. Dr. Holland
had brought his wife to call at the Dickinson home one day,
and Emily and Mrs. Holland had liked one another
immediately. Mrs. Holland was older than Emily, but the
two began a happy and stimulating friendship that lasted
their lifetime. They visited one another occasionally, and in
their frequent letters Mrs. Holland became "Sister" to
Emily.

Renovations on the Dickinson homestead were completed
by the end of 1855. The family moved in during January.
Despite such welcome improvements as pump water right
in the kitchen sink and a glass conservatory built onto the
dining room to house Emily's flowers, the Dickinsons bade
the big white North Pleasant Street house a reluctant good-
bye. They had spent fifteen happy years there. Just to the
west of the Main Street mansion rose Austin and Sue's
new home.

> *One Sister have I in our house,*
> *And one, a hedge away.*
> *There's only one recorded,*
> *But both belong to me.*
>
> *One came the road that I came—*
> *And wore my last year's gown—*
> *The other, as a bird her nest,*
> *Builded our hearts among.*

With loving verse Emily greeted Sue's entrance into the family. By way of marriage and the acceptance of a man's responsibilities, Austin had grown up. Emily still hesitated before the experience of womanhood. Finely balanced in suspended girlhood, she was reluctant to leave its safety. A forward step would mean exposure to the dangers inherent in adult life.

Five

Between the mansion and the Austin Dickinson home stretched a narrow dirt path connecting the back door of one house with the back door of the other. The path had been made by Dickinsons, by Austin walking over to consult his father on legal matters, by Emily, Vinnie, and Sue exchanging visits, by Squire Dickinson striding purposefully next door to drink a cup of strong tea with his daughter-in-law, by Mrs. Dickinson scurrying cross-lots with soups and custards. The path survived encroaching summer grasses and obliterating winter snowfalls. It was used many times a day.

One bright cold winter night in early 1859 Emily was taking the path. Light from an almost full moon glistened on deep, crusted snow. The footing was treacherous. Footprints made when the sun was high had frozen into slippery ruts. Emily kept a gloved hand on Carlo's brown neck and with his support accomplished her journey safely.

Earlier in the day Sue had sent word that she and her house guest, a friend named Kate Scott, would be at home that evening before a cozy fire and they were hoping Emily would join them. Emily decided to go.

She did not always accept invitations so readily. Many evenings when the gaily glittering lights of Sue's drawing room illuminated Amherst friends and visitors engaged in lively conversation, Emily, although invited, preferred to remain at home.

Shyness had always been part of her make-up. Now she exhibited decided reticence about going into public. Emily liked the familiar shelter of her own home and the companionship of a few friends, chosen principally from her own family circle. She left the Dickinson grounds only to go to church or to one or two other houses in Amherst, but avoided even church when she could manage it. It wasn't only that she found Church doctrine too militant for her tastes. The stares of people in the congregation distressed her. She preferred to seek the minister in his own home.

Emily excused herself as old-fashioned, and her manner

did appear a little quaint. She was direct and unpretentious and warmly loving toward her friends. But in public, reticence overcame her normally open, affectionate nature, causing an emotional turmoil Emily found difficult to govern. It was the reason she preferred intimate surroundings to crowded drawing rooms. She sought small audiences. A single listener, or at the most two, would do.

With dignity and solidarity the Dickinsons accepted Emily's peculiarities, although Father and Austin reprimanded her when her ways bordered on rudeness. They could not always forgive her habit of hiding from guests who came to call. Emily hung her head and acknowledged herself a "felon, sentenced for a door bell," but did not change her ways. She didn't mean to injure the feelings of visitors, but only to protect her own.

Sue's friend Kate Scott was not one from whom Emily ran away. Pretty, bright, full of fun, yet not unacquainted with sorrow, Kate dressed in mourning for the husband she had lost two years earlier. Emily was drawn to her, and the two were becoming fast friends.

That evening spent in front of Sue's fire passed happily. The three young women sewed and talked and laughed with girlish high spirits, enjoying one another's company immensely. Emily so forgot herself and the time that she was as startled as the others to hear a loud thumping of boots in the back entry. A moment later Father, looking stern and tired, appeared in the doorway with his lantern. It seemed to him high time his elder daughter was home in bed. Emily might have been fifteen years old instead of almost thirty.

Most evenings Emily spent a different way. Her custom of settling at her writing stand after the rest of the family retired had become confirmed habit. In her room in the upper southwest corner of the mansion, she wrote many of her letters and secretly worked at writing verse.

She was far from satisfied with her early attempts at poetry, most of which she later discarded because they seemed too conventional or too sentimental. Emily found it hard to avoid being sentimental. In her early flush of desire to become a poet she had indulged in flowery writing. Then, too, much of the contemporary literature she read was so mawkish and emotionally excessive that its tone occasionally crept unnoticed into her writing, though she made every effort now to keep it out and record only honest emotion.

Emily's greatest aid in writing was her well-thumbed dictionary. She intensely desired to express her thoughts precisely, and consulted the lexicon endlessly to find exactly the word she wanted to convey just the meaning she intended.

Constant practice in writing with scrupulous honesty was resulting in better poems. She was more thoroughly disciplined now in the use of words, in the manipulation of meters, in her ability to pin her thoughts succinctly on paper.

More and more of her poems pleased her enough that she saved them. She began making little booklets by folding several pieces of writing paper and binding them with a few large stitches of white thread. In the booklets she transcribed her best poems, once she had polished them to her satisfaction. By 1859 some seventy-five poems were entered in a growing collection of booklets hidden in her bottom bureau drawer.

The themes she treated were those that naturally occupied her thoughts. Friendship, nature, and death were subjects she wrote about constantly. Her interest in death at times seemed morbid, at times sentimental, but it was always real. Since Ben Newton's dying, her concern with the grave had amounted almost to an obsession. One poem after another puzzled about the phenomenon. "That *Bareheaded life*— under the grass—worries one like a Wasp," she admitted to a friend.

Occasionally Emily Dickinson's poems provided glimpses of her intimate feelings, although she warned readers that "when I state myself, as the Representative of the Verse— it does not mean—me—but a supposed person." No one knew better than Emily what was denied her by her confined life, and by what she termed her "cowardice of strangers." There were inevitably despairing moments when she wished she were otherwise constituted.

> *I never hear the word "escape"*
> *Without a quicker blood,*
> *A sudden expectation,*
> *A flying attitude!*
>
> *I never hear of prisons broad*
> *By soldiers battered down,*
> *But I tug childish at my bars*
> *Only to fail again!*

As the number of poems saved in her bureau mounted, Emily increasingly felt the need for critical guidance in her work. She yearned for the help of someone who could capably appraise her efforts. At first she quite naturally turned to Sue, for her sister-in-law read widely and her literary judgment was sound. Sue shared Emily's interest in intellectual pursuits. It was the strongest bond between them.

Emily sent many verses across to the other house to elicit Sue's comments. Sue praised Emily's efforts or offered constructive criticism. But though Sue's mind might keep pace with Emily's, it could not lead it. Emily knew she needed a mind that mastered hers. She had found a master once in Ben Newton. Would she find another?

About the time that Emily's poems were beginning to accumulate, the Dickinsons made a new friend. Samuel Bowles, the handsome, vital editor of the *Springfield Republican,* was close to Austin Dickinson's age. The two men met and quickly became friends. Beginning about 1858 Sam Bowles frequently visited the Dickinsons in Amherst, occasionally, in the beginning, bringing his wife with him.

Mr. Bowles possessed lively intelligence, wide-ranging enthusiasms, and quick imagination, all of which had helped make his newspaper one of the foremost in the nation. His interest in politics, literature, travel, and world-wide events were reflected in the columns he published. Beyond this, Samuel Bowles naturally liked and enjoyed people. He numbered among his close friends many men and women of ability and intelligence.

As one of the circle caught up in admiration for Austin's new friend, Emily, too, was drawn to Samuel Bowles. His familiarity with the world from which she instinctively withdrew, the broad scope of his interests, and the warmth and compassion of his nature may have led Emily to hope that in him she had found a new preceptor.

However, Samuel Bowles had a limitation upon his life. He was frail in health, forced to guard carefully against overextending his energies in the course of his busy career.

He would have had neither strength nor time to sustain the intense relationship Emily desired.

That Emily actually did ask him to guide and teach her is no more than speculation, but about 1858 she wrote a peculiarly defiant poem.

> *I never lost as much but twice,*
> *And that was in the sod.*
> *Twice have I stood a beggar*
> *Before the door of God!*
>
> *Angels—twice descending*
> *Reimbursed my store—*
> *Burglar! Banker—Father!*
> *I am poor once more!*

Death had twice robbed her of beloved teachers, first Amherst Academy Principal Leonard Humphrey, then Ben Newton. Perhaps with this verse Emily buried her hopes that Samuel Bowles might be a third.

Nevertheless, Emily and Mr. Bowles, as she always called him, became warm friends. Correspondence flourished between them. He dubbed Emily his Queen Recluse, and no one else succeeded as he did in penetrating the defenses she set up to protect herself. Probably no one else of Samuel Bowles's acquaintance plied him with such unconventional observations as, "Summer stopped since you were here. Nobody noticed her—that is, no men and women. Doubtless, the fields are rent by petite anguish, and 'mourners go about' the Woods."

Emily easily personified nature in her letters and poems because she loved it and lived consciously close to it. Nature provided her a key to the secrets of life, and in its annual revolution she recognized the age-old pattern of birth, death, and rebirth.

A century ago, rural New England communities like Amherst were gently tuned to the ever-recurring cycle of the seasons. In winter, deep snow and penetrating cold kept people close to the warmth of kitchen fires and parlor stoves. While on crisp, sparkling days, youngsters took to local hills with sleds, and horse-drawn, bell-jingling sleighs ran over snow-packed highways, the complete picture of a New England winter bears testimony to days of dismal gray skies, waking hours spent in ill-lighted darkness, long stretches of routine broken occasionally by lectures and quiet social affairs. After thirty-five years' experience with leaden days, Emily would note,

> *The Sky is low—the Clouds are mean.*
> *A Travelling Flake of Snow*
> *Across a Barn or through a Rut*
> *Debates if it will go—*

A Narrow Wind complains all Day
How some one treated him
Nature, like Us is sometimes caught
Without her Diadem.

Emily characterized March as the long-awaited guest. She loved the spring. Her spirits lightened as sap ran in the sugar maples, and melting snow and ice turned frozen soil to thick, sticky, ubiquitous mud. "Infinite March is here, and I 'hered' a bluebird. Of course I am standing on my head!"

Spring was a time for readying. Yards were tidied, gardens uncovered, vines and fruit trees trimmed, manure gotten out, wood neatly repiled. As the weather warmed, doors opened, dust flew out, sunlight streamed in, and the steady round of visits and attentions that were the mainstay of a small town's social activity were undertaken with renewed energy. Carrying a glass of jelly, flowers, or a bit of news, ladies like Mrs. Dickinson set forth almost daily to visit friends and neighbors and to do their Christian duty by the sick, the aged, and the low-spirited.

During the lazy summer Amherst farmers swung their scythes in the hayfields and hoed among the corn rows. Bees droned in the clover and butterflies squandered their brief lives in the tall meadow grasses. Emily and Vinnie Dickinson cultivated a handsome flower garden in the mansion's side yard. Both enjoyed gardening, but Emily possessed the exquisite touch. Under her care the most delicate wildflower thrived; lilies, heliotrope, and cape jasmine grew to perfect bloom. Lovingly she watched her blossoms through their life cycles. Even the bumblebees that visited the columbine and the spiders that spun among the delphinium leaves did not escape her surveillance.

Several holidays occurred during the summer. On Annual Muster Day in June the Amherst militia paraded on the southern stretch of common and provided great local excitement, especially among the town's small-boy population. The Fourth of July and Amherst College commencement in August were other highlights. For several years now Edward Dickinson had held a tea at his home on the day preceding the college graduation ceremonies. Seniors, faculty, trustees, and visiting dignitaries attended the event. Its success rapidly made the Dickinson Commencement Tea an established part of the annual traditions.

At harvest time, when local crops yielded to gathering hands, the Dickinson larder was replenished by homegrown rosy, golden peaches, juicy purple grapes, handsome apples, and sweet cider. Fall became a season of perpetual motion, with bright falling leaves, flocks of migrating birds, and returning students all contributing to the kaleidoscopic effect. Emily commemorated the brief lull created by October's Indian summer with a poem.

These are the days when Birds come back—
A very few—a Bird or two—
To take a backward look.

These are the days when skies resume
The old—old sophistries of June—
A blue and gold mistake.

Oh fraud that cannot cheat the Bee—
Almost thy plausibility
Induces my belief.

Till ranks of seeds their witness bear—
And softly thro' the altered air
Hurries a timid leaf.

Oh Sacrament of summer days,
Oh Last Communion in the Haze—
Permit a child to join.

Thy sacred emblems to partake—
Thy consecrated bread to take
And thine immortal wine!

October was also the time of Amherst's annual Cattle Show, to which farmers from miles about brought their best stock and produce, and for which local housewives baked pies and fancied up their most delectable jellies. Dickinsons were always involved in the event. If Edward Dickinson wasn't displaying the prize-winning carriage horse, Austin was judging the fruits and vegetables, or Emily was taking a ribbon for her loaf of Indian and rye bread.

The days grew shorter and colder. Stoves were set in the bedrooms and parlors. After Thanksgiving passed, winter descended once more. This seasonal pattern, repeated again and again, eventually became so real to Emily Dickinson that each month took on a singular personality.

Her life, as she reached the age of thirty, appeared outwardly uneventful. She cooked, she sewed, she gardened, and spent leisure hours writing letters, playing the piano, and reading. Emily's love of books was a paramount passion in her life. Her "kinsmen of the shelf" were dear to her as friends were dear, and with them she sought stimulus and release. Shakespeare and Dickens, Keats and Ruskin, Sir Thomas Browne, and the Bible's Book of Revelations she listed as favorites. In these writings she found passages to love and cadences to absorb into her own experience. Among other contemporary books she was drawn to the works of Charlotte and Emily Brontë, the novels of George Eliot, and the poems of Elizabeth Barrett Browning and her husband, Robert Browning. What books and magazines escaped Emily's notice were likely to be caught by Sue, whose library table held the most widely discussed current literature.

Father still objected to the books Emily indulged in. One early morning he surprised her in the kitchen reading a new novel by Herman Melville while the potatoes warmed for breakfast. An hour later Father read aloud from the family Bible the parable of the servant who buried the talent given him by his master, rather than putting it to profitable use. The message did not escape Emily.

The incident was another example of how Father's "real life" and Emily's still collided, just as they always had. To Father life was duty—civic duty, moral duty, religious duty, duty in a hundred forms, all waiting to be shouldered and diligently carried out.

To Emily life was something else, an experience so vast and so unfathomable that she was only just testing the shallows, had not yet begun to explore the greater depths. She felt that life was something more than the Church's formula of time spent striving for the next world. She knew life when she met it, whether in the stirring thoughts encountered in books or in the smaller happenings of her own quiet existence. Emily's goal in her poems was to tell the truth about this great unknown as she experienced it.

> *Surgeons must be very careful*
> *When they take the knife!*
> *Underneath their fine incisions*
> *Stirs the Culprit—Life!*

How confounding that culprit was Emily Dickinson well knew. The tools with which she conducted her surgery were wit, joy in manipulating language to fit her thoughts, and sensitivity to being alive. Emily was determined to explore the great mysterious quality called life.

The images that were appearing most frequently in her poems were bumblebees and butterflies, sunsets and sparrows, and many other natural phenomena. Emily chose them because she knew them intimately. Later in life she would use such words as awe and bliss and immortality as familiarly as birds and rainbows, but now she knew the natural world best and spoke her message in its terminology.

The images from nature were appropriate in another way, too, for many of them were scaled to Emily Dickinson's unique sense of proportion. With her keen sensitivity, Emily could take heady delight in a flower bursting into bloom in her conservatory, find adventure in sending her thoughts in a letter. Small creatures, small happenings, had large significance. Her emblem might well have been the sparrow of one of her poems, which found a sovereign existence in its crumb.

Her consistent use of the common phenomena of nature suggests, too, Emily's predilection for the known and the familiar as refuge against the mysterious in life. Death, for instance, was one of life's incomprehensible and therefore terrifying forces. In poem after poem Emily tried to understand what death was, but could not penetrate the curtain that separated it from life.

She could find no assurance of an afterlife. She sought, but could not find, evidence of a loving God whose superior power gave meaning to the world. Instinctively, therefore, she clung to such visible order as the patterns perceptible in nature, as the quiet routine within the parental home. When ordered life was upset in any of a dozen ways, Emily Dickinson became gloomy and despairing. At such times she acknowledged herself "at sea."

During the year 1860 Emily was frequently at sea. Bothered by poor health throughout the early months of that year, she was further afflicted in the spring by the death of Aunt Lavinia Norcross, Mrs. Dickinson's favorite sister and the aunt closest to the Dickinson children. She had been ill for over a year, and though her recovery could not be hoped for, her death deeply saddened all the Dickinsons.

Emily was upset, too, by the long absence of her beloved Vinnie, who had spent many weeks in Boston helping the Norcross family through its time of trouble. Lavinia acted more and more as buffer between Emily and the practical problems and inconveniences of life.

By the time of commencement in August, however, Emily's spirits were restored. The graduation festivities, which Emily normally dreaded, seemed this year more gala than usual. Amherst was crowded with visitors from out of town, some of them interesting newcomers, many of them old friends of the college and the townspeople.

Governor Banks and his wife were guests of the Edward Dickinsons. From the time the governor's party arrived on the Wednesday afternoon train, the mansion was thrown into a flurry of excitement. Messages flew back and forth between the two Dickinson houses. Could Sue spare a loaf of unsliced bread? Emily had been silly enough to cut six for the Commencement Tea when she needed only three and now had no whole loaves left. Both houses teemed with visitors. The half-orphaned daughters of Aunt Lavinia, Louise and Fanny Norcross, were established at Austin's. There, too, was Emily and Vinnie's friend Eliza Coleman, who had moved now from Philadelphia to Middletown, Connecticut, and was brought to Amherst by her fiancé, the Reverend John Dudley.

As the hour appointed for the Dickinson Commencement Tea neared, students, faculty members, and out-of-town guests, men and women in their summer best, strolled through the dappled sunlight toward the Dickinson mansion. Horse-drawn vehicles lined both sides of the street near the entrance to the homestead. The big front door stood open, permitting people to flow in and out of the stately brick house. Inside, as well as out on the lawn, were long tables holding bread and butter, punch and tea, ices and cakes. The long skirts of the ladies swept across the new-mown grass, and colorful parasols dipped and twirled in Emily's garden.

Emily scurried breathlessly among the guests, speaking shyly with one or another, finding small kitchen errands to perform when the crowd grew too overwhelming. She caught sight of Samuel Bowles at the center of an animated group and could see that Eliza was shepherding the Norcross cousins, who must find so much commotion startling.

Emily was caught up in talking to a tall, thin, uniformed man who introduced himself as Major Hunt. He was the husband of vivacious Helen Fiske, an Amherst girl Emily had known slightly years before at the Amherst Academy, but who had not been in town for a long time. Major Hunt was watching Carlo wander among the multitude of legs, canes, and skirts. The big dog kept purposefully close to the food-laden tables and from time to time was able to snap up a cake knocked accidentally to the grass.

"I think your dog understands gravitation," said the amused major.

The remark delighted Emily.

John Dudley, Eliza Coleman's fiancé, interested her, too. He was forty-eight years old and had been pastor of the Middletown, Connecticut, Congregational Church for ten years. He was said to be very liberal in his views. Emily came to know him better in October when she and Vinnie visited the Colemans' home in Middletown.

Excitement so infected Emily this commencement that very late Thursday night, after the ceremonies at the college were concluded, she sat at her writing table composing an apology to Samuel Bowles. Emily, feeling unusually gay, had engaged him in a discussion about women. Samuel Bowles held women in higher esteem than Emily did. She was convinced that many of her own sex possessed "muslin souls" and "Dimity Convictions." She had been witty, but she also had been a bit giddy, and now she begged Mr. Bowles's forgiveness for having "smiled at women." For certain women Emily had great respect. They were the Florence Nightingales and Elizabeth Barrett Brownings, who did not hide behind their femininity but made effective use of their talents.

Emily Dickinson knew periods of happiness and of unhappiness during 1860. That same year she encountered an entirely new experience. She was, at thirty, a tiny woman with a strikingly original mind and shy, sensitive, eager manner. She had won a small reputation for her intelligence and her wit. She was not pretty. Secretly she was working at becoming a poet, and quietly she was searching for someone to guide her to that goal. At some time during 1860 Emily met a man with whom she fell in love.

An aura of mystery will probably always cloud the event, for nowhere in the immense collection of poems and letters which have survived her did Emily mention the name of the man she loved. And he did not love her in return. Clues concerning his identity can be traced to several men whose lives touched hers about the year 1860. Whether her heart selected one of these or some other may never be known. The evidence is too thin to support the case for any one candidate, but curiosity has been sustained over the decades for the simple reason that Emily's thwarted love affair brought on the flood of her genius. From the experience was born a poet.

Up to the year 1860 Emily had carefully copied 150 poems into the paper packets she contrived of notepaper and thread. During the following six years she entered close to a thousand poems. The equivalent of one a day, 365 of them, are attributed to the single year 1862.

Since Emily never dated her poems or her letters, dates have been assigned her verses and her correspondence by scholars who have made prolonged study of the changes in her handwriting, of the references in the letters to actual events, and of the general tenor of her manuscripts. The work of fitting together the pieces of her life has been an intriguing, but frequently baffling, scholastic jigsaw puzzle. Many assumptions about Emily Dickinson's writing must still be based on circumstantial evidence rather than on fact.

The incredible number of poems she wrote between 1860 and 1865 is evidence of an immense flow of emotion that occurred in her life. The contents of the poems reveal the intensity of that flow. Until 1860 her poetry had been concerned with life and death, with nature and self-knowledge. Now all she wrote related in some way to the enormous, unfathomed new category, love.

Once, at the time of Benjamin Newton's demise, Emily had found that "Death was as much of Mob as I could master." Now she was mobbed by love, and she struggled desperately to remain in control.

It is not difficult to trace in the poetry the story of a love that blooms, is blighted, and eventually becomes reconciled to its fate. The danger lies in reading too much into the lines Emily Dickinson committed to paper, in being tempted to learn facts from her distilled thought, for the poet's style is so forthright and honest that it seems to belie the distillation process. Emily's lifelong passion for truth is simply and clearly exhibited. There is no pretention in her verse. Her concern is for the truth at the core of her experience, and her poems succinctly and baldly expose her emotions.

Emily Dickinson achieved such economy of expression that sometimes the essence of her poems is condensed into the single first line. In many of her verses her message is stated in the first quatrain, with subsequent lines serving only for swift illustration. Her poems are rarely long, her artistry almost never diluted by extended images or unnecessary verbiage. The meters she chose, the rhythms that came most naturally, were frequently those of church hymns, whose cadences she had learned during childhood.

That Emily Dickinson wrote with such control at a time when much of the poetry being written and published by others was effusive, sentimental and lengthy, isolates her work. But that she could exercise artistic mastery over the song that burst from her in moments of despair and longing, or again at times of great excitement and anticipation, reveals her genius. Her expressions of deep feeling, flung freely from overwrought sensibilities, do not trespass upon excess. The years spent in training to be a poet had not been wasted.

Emily's love affair can be sketched briefly by looking at poems that represent its progressive stages. Among the enraptured verses she wrote the year she fell in love, the year she hoped, is this:

> *'Tis so much joy! 'Tis so much joy!*
> *If I should fail, what poverty!*
> *And yet, as poor as I,*
> *Have ventured all upon a throw!*
> *Have gained! Yes! Hesitated so—*
> *This side the Victory!*
>
> *Life is but Life! And Death, but Death!*
> *Bliss is but Bliss, and Breath but Breath!*
> *And if indeed I fail,*

At least, to know the worst, is sweet!
Defeat means nothing but Defeat,
No drearier, can befall!

And if I gain! Oh Gun at Sea!
Oh Bells, that in the Steeples be!
At first, repeat it slow!
For Heaven is a different thing,
Conjectured, and waked sudden in—
And might extinguish me!

With or without encouragement from the man she loved, Emily envisioned herself his bride. She wrote several poems in which she represented herself dressed in white. One of these she sent to Mr. Bowles, whose friendship she depended upon more heavily than any other. He is possibly the only person in whom she confided the secret of her heart's dilemma.

Sometime during 1861 Emily learned the crushing truth that she was not desired by the man she loved. The news was deeply shocking. In deadly echo to the resonances of the earlier verse is this stark poem in which Emily Dickinson has come face to face with the grimmest reality of her life:

'Tis so appalling—it exhilirates—
So over Horror, it half Captivates—

The Soul stares after it, secure—
To know the worst, leaves no dread more.

The depth of the wound Emily sustained can be gauged by listing a few first lines among the hundreds of poems she poured upon paper. "The nearest dream recedes unrealized," "Not in this world to see his face," "We grow accustomed to the dark," "More life went out when he went," "I live with him—I see his face," are but a few of her cries of agony.

Her despair very nearly overwhelmed her, and there are hints in the poems and letters she wrote during the months that followed that she came to fear for her reason. If dread of insanity *was* an added burden, Emily's plight was close to desperate. More than one critic has suggested that only by the discipline of channeling her chaotic emotions into poetry did she keep off madness.

The most revealing statement from Emily herself is in a letter written during the spring of 1862. "I had a terror—since September—I could tell to none—and so I sing, as the Boy does by the Burying Ground—because I am afraid."

Life seemed blackest to Emily during that spring. In the midst of emotional crisis she was losing two of her dearest friends. The Reverend Charles Wadsworth of Philadelphia, with whom Emily had corresponded concerning spiritual matters, and whose aid she had sought during the current turmoil, decided to leave his Arch Street Presbyterian Church to become pastor of Calvary Church in San Francisco. Sometime during 1860 Charles Wadsworth had visited nearby Northampton and had made a trip to Amherst to call on Emily Dickinson. Forty-six years old at the time and married, he was dressed in mourning for his mother's recent death. There has been considerable speculation that he was the man with whom Emily Dickinson fell in love. He departed for the West in early May, 1862.

Samuel Bowles, whose health had been poor since the preceding autumn, decided to try a complete change of scene for remedy, and accordingly left for a seven-month trip to Europe in early April, 1862. In one man Emily was losing her spiritual advisor, in the other her worldly confidant. Although she could still write to them, her mind had ever equated distance and death, and undoubtedly she felt as bereft as if the two men had left the earth.

In addition Emily was coping with the incredible outpouring of poetry. There was within her a desperate need to know whether these products of her private anguish were, as she dared believe, poetry. A mind skirting the abyss of irrationality would need to know, and would seek the verdict of a qualified, impartial source.

Almost like a sign from heaven there appeared in the April, 1862, issue of the *Atlantic Monthly* an article entitled, "Letter to a Young Contributor." It was an essay of advice and precepts for unpublished writers by a New Englander named Thomas Wentworth Higginson. Higginson was a frequent contributor to the *Atlantic Monthly*. Emily knew his style and knew his interest in abolition and women's rights. "Letter to a Young Contributor" counseled would-be authors about their literary manners, their style, their aspirations. If Mr. Higginson really hoped, as he suggested early in his essay, to bring to light new literary talent, he had the incredible fortune of finding that talent on his first try. Emily Dickinson accepted his invitation by responding at once.

"Mr. Higginson,
   Are you too deeply occupied to say if my Verse is alive?
   The Mind is so near itself—it cannot see, distinctly—and I have none to ask—Should you think it breathed—and had you the leisure to tell me, I should feel quick gratitude. . . ."

Her letter was short. She did not sign her name, but enclosed a handwritten calling card. She also enclosed four poems.

Wentworth Higginson answered right away. Although his letters to Emily Dickinson have not survived, he seems to have both praised and criticized her poems. He asked to see more of her work, and evidently was curious to know who she was, what she looked like, what her education had been, and what authors she admired, for Emily parried these questions in the correspondence that followed. Most importantly, he treated her verses as serious poetry.

Emily's poems seem to have struck Mr. Higginson as strong, startlingly beautiful, and completely unorthodox. Surely they met in every respect the precepts he had outlined in his article. The verse was polished, its phrases carefully selected, its thought economical, its message incisive and true. But the liberties Emily took with meter and rhyme dumbfounded him. Imagine rhyming "time" with "ran" and calling the poem finished! Mr. Higginson did not feel the reading public would accept that as poetry. He recommended that she put off attempting to publish.

Publication was not her aim, Emily assured him. But she did need a friend and teacher to guide her. Would Mr. Higginson be her preceptor? Mr. Higginson evidently said he would, and years later Emily told him he had saved her life. Though he had quibbled with her rhymes and spellings, he had not questioned her achievement as a poet.

During the very time of crisis in Emily Dickinson's life the nation was experiencing a great crisis of its own in civil war. The first guns were fired at Fort Sumter on April 12, 1861, but enmity and conflict had been building between North and South for many years before.

News of the outbreak of war brought greater excitement

to Amherst than to many another New England town because of the Amherst College students. Young, filled with enthusiasm and idealism, and anticipating that the strife would be swift and glorious, they were eager to leave college at President Lincoln's first call for volunteers. On the morning of April 21, after listening to a stirring sermon by Professor Tyler concerning war and patriotism, the students were so roused that when young chemistry professor William Clark stood on the steps of the chapel and declared he would lead a company of one hundred men against the South, one hundred students enlisted with him on the spot.

With the students astir, the whole town rippled with urgency and anticipation. The usually peaceful streets were filled until long after dark each day with men discussing, arguing, planning. The college faculty prevailed upon the students to stay until commencement, although several Southern boys left for home at once. For the first time in the college's history, commencement was held in early July that year, with no festivities except President Stearns's levee for seniors to mark the occasion. After the students left, the Civil War seemed farther away from Amherst.

It was brought close again in less than a year. The Union Army, having suffered defeat after defeat during the first eleven months of war, at last won a victory at New Bern, North Carolina, on March 14, 1862. The news brought little cheer to Amherst, for with it came word that young

Frazar Stearns, son of the Amherst College President, was dead. He was not the first Amherst man to die, but he was one of the town's best-loved, most promising youths, and was a symbol of that band of heroes who had marched off bravely in Professor Clark's company the summer before.

"Austin is chilled—by Frazer's murder," reported Emily to Samuel Bowles. "He says—his Brain keeps saying over 'Frazer is killed'—'Frazer is killed,' just as Father told it—to Him. Two or three words of lead—that dropped so deep, they keep weighing—"

Frazar's body was brought home in a wooden box by one of his soldier classmates. The townspeople covered his coffin with flowers, students walked beside him to the graveyard. Amherst felt it had paid a high price to the war, and looked for the strife to be over soon. But there were three long years yet to go.

Emily Dickinson, who rarely commented in her writing on national events, felt in the Civil War the large echo of her own unhappiness. "Sorrow seems more general than it did, and not the estate of a few persons, since the war began," she wrote to Louise and Fanny Norcross, adding, ". . . if the anguish of others helped one with one's own, now would be many medicines."

Time and exhausting struggle finally ended the Civil War. Time and the ability to endure were the anodynes that soothed Emily's grief. Gradually, during 1863 and the years that followed, Emily recovered from her painful experience. The hurt never entirely subsided. Years later she would still lay blame to "that old nail in my breast" as a source of troubled spirit.

One poem, written toward the end of her period of crisis, stands as special tribute to a being to whom Emily directed her devotion.

> *Of all the Souls that stand create—*
> *I have elected—One—*
> *When Sense from Spirit—files away—*
> *And Subterfuge—is done—*
> *When that which is—and that which was—*
> *Apart—intrinsic—stand—*
> *And this brief Tragedy of Flesh—*
> *Is shifted—like a Sand—*
> *When Figures show their royal Front—*
> *And Mists—are carved away,*
> *Behold the Atom—I preferred—*
> *To all the lists of Clay!*

Whether the atom she preferred was the man she loved or, as critics have suggested, God, the poem conveys the message that the poet has made a choice, that she has turned inward toward a single image and has closed "the Valves of her attention" to others. In actuality she did turn inward.

When the period of emotional upheaval was over, Emily completed her hesitant withdrawal from society, and afterward did not leave the Dickinson property. In addition she began the unusual habit of wearing only white dresses, as if she had dedicated herself to some one or some thing.

Two final exceptions to her voluntary retirement occurred during 1864 and 1865 when a prolonged and troublesome eye ailment caused her to go to Boston for treatment. For many months she lived quietly in the city with Lou and Fanny Norcross, forbidden reading or writing by her physician.

As Emily Dickinson's emotional turbulence calmed, the great seizure of poetry-writing quieted significantly. She continued to write poetry, but the rapid pace at which she composed it slowed. After 1865 she completed about twenty poems each year.

Her years of turmoil had been strenuous, but she had survived. Years later she summed her experience.

> *I should not dare to be so sad*
> *So many Years again—*
> *A Load is first impossible*
> *When we have put it down—*
>
> *The Superhuman then withdraws*
> *And we who never saw*

> *The Giant at the other side*
> *Begin to perish now.*

Emerging from the period of intense unhappiness, her attention was absorbed by other great themes which she began to command with her poetic resources.

Six

"Ned! Ned! Hurry! There's a storm coming!"

"Ready about, then. We'll head for Portugal."

"Aye, aye, sir. Hard a'lee!"

The children were playing on the Dickinson grounds. Behind the sturdy picket fence and the hedges their high-pitched chatter and laughter sounded all the balmy summer morning. Young, strident voices penetrated the open windows of the mansion and the Austin Dickinson home.

Four children, Ned and Mattie Dickinson, Did and Mac Jenkins, were enacting a drama of sailing, shipwreck, and struggle for survival that took them back and forth across the long-grassed lawn, along the shrubbery, beneath the tall evergreens and through the orchard. Using the laundry basket for a boat and sticks for weapons, the children made unerring if devious progress toward the southwest corner of the mansion. Beneath a certain window they abandoned all hope and loudly gave themselves up to starvation.

To their joy the expiring youngsters had not long to wait for rescue. The low rumble of an upstairs window cautiously being raised announced the arrival of help. The children glimpsed a white-clothed figure. A woven basket appeared upon the stone sill. Two hands played out a length of sturdy twine attached to its handle, and the basket rode faultlessly to the ground. The youngsters descended upon the basket eagerly, plundered its contents, and bore their booty to a retreat behind the syringa bushes.

Their prize was four oval cakes of gingerbread, golden and crisp on the exterior, soft, spicy and chewy within. Experienced consumers of the neighborhood's baked products, the children recognized that the gingerbread had been made by Miss Emily. Within five minutes not a crumb remained.

Ned and Mattie Dickinson were Austin and Sue's children. Did and Mac Jenkins belonged to the Reverend Jonathan Jenkins, the newest minister to occupy the pulpit of First Church. There was a new pulpit for Mr. Jenkins to occupy, for the members of the First Congregational Church had recently built a new gray stone meetinghouse on Main Street, across from Austin Dickinson's home. Austin himself had headed the building committee. When the Jenkins family moved into the adjacent new parsonage they rapidly became good friends with the Dickinsons.

Although the assorted ages of the children left a wide gap between Ned, the oldest, and Mac, the youngest, the four youngsters were companions. Together they roamed Amherst's meadows and woodlots, explored barns and carriage sheds, were familiar with surrounding cow pastures, chicken coops, and woodpiles. They were bounded only by the limits of their imaginations and the restrictions placed upon them by their elders. An important niche in their world was occupied by Emily Dickinson.

There were things known to the children about Miss Emily that were every bit as fascinating as the fact that the church sexton wore a wig and a glass eye. For one thing, Ned and Mattie's Aunt Emily dressed invariably in white, winter or summer. For another, she never left her father's property. When she was younger, they knew, she had appeared in the village and its environs as normally as anyone else, but by her own choice she preferred now to be nowhere but in her own house or garden.

Furthermore, very few people outside the Dickinson family ever saw her. She was inaccessible to almost all. A very few old and once-intimate friends occasionally called on her by appointment, but even then Miss Emily might decline to see them, sending down from her room a delicately worded note of apology, or from her garden a flower, which Maggie, the Dickinson maid, would carry to the disappointed visitor. If surprised in the kitchen by the unexpected arrival at the back door of a neighbor or the grocery boy, Miss Emily disappeared quick as a flash into the pantry passage. She was more wary than a chipmunk.

People in the village who weren't intimate with the Dickinsons did not know what to make of the Squire's daughter's odd ways. They heard she was brilliant, that she wrote poetry. Neighbors mentioned beautifully phrased notes of thank you or sympathy sent them upon occasion from the mansion. But such a strong desire for seclusion seemed peculiar in the daughter of Amherst's most prominent citizen. For lack of any other explanation many in Amherst called her queer. She made them curious. They tried to glimpse her tiny white figure as they passed Squire Dickinson's hedge.

The children who played with Ned and Mattie knew Miss Emily wasn't queer in the sense that town gossips meant it. She was different, but in a way the children found beautiful. She was tiny and shy, with a mass of red-brown hair and dancing eyes. Her voice was low and pleasant, and she spoke in an exciting, compelling way. She seemed always poised for flight, yet did not fly from children. Rather she fully enjoyed their candor, their directness, the comical feats accomplished by their imaginations. When children came to the mansion on errands Miss Emily would sometimes appear and talk to them. She welcomed the wild-flowers they brought and the secrets they confided. Once she shared with one of them her thrill in watching a moth emerge from chrysalis in her conservatory.

Emily Dickinson's delight in children was fostered by her own lively imagination. When Ned, as a small boy, insisted that the kitten ticked and the clock purred, Emily smiled. "He inherits his Uncle Emily's ardor for the lie," she said.

Children recognized in Emily Dickinson an ally, although no common one. Their interviews were too rare, Miss Emily's ways too unusual, for that. But it was she, of all the grown-ups they knew, who best understood the problems children face in an adult-governed world. Her short notes, scrawled quickly in an almost unreadable hand, brought solace and humorous sympathy to young culprits at the darkest moments. Although her cryptic message might mystify the boy or girl who received it, it was usually put away and saved among his treasures.

Emily now lived an existence entirely bounded by Dick-insons and hemlock hedges. By choice she had retired from direct contact with the world. By choice, but also by necessity, for she was so fully occupied by her life within the mansion that she had no time to spare.

Living had become for her "a Bliss so powerful—we must die—to adjust it." She had emerged from the blackest period of her life triumphant in the knowledge that she was a poet. The role gave her courage to confront the unknown. She probed the experience of life to discover its most profound secrets.

The more her thought matured, the more complicated and less solvable seemed her abiding concern with God's identity and with the relationship between life on earth and that in the world to come. By their very nature these would always remain mysteries. Yet Emily persisted in her search for meanings, piecing together the baffling clues provided her by daily existence.

She had chosen a word to sum the substance of her preoccupation. The word was *circumference*. She did not use circumference in the strict sense of limitation, but thought of it as that which surrounds, as the glow of light surrounds the wick of a burning candle.

Circumference was to her an area of meanings radiating outward from an idea, a concept, a happening, from life itself. Some of circumference was knowable, some unknowable. But as a poet she sought to explore it and comprehend its meanings. "Perhaps you smile at me," she wrote to her literary friend, Thomas Wentworth Higginson. "I could not stop for that—My Business is Circumference."

Living in seclusion Emily devoted herself to studying circumference, puzzling the relationships that love and hope, joy and deprivation bore in the scheme of living and dying. Her discoveries she recorded in her poems and letters.

One area she probed continually was the nature of the force that governed life. She found evidence in everyday circumstances of a superior power, although its secret continued to elude her. But she was still as skeptical as ever of the personable image of God presented by the Congregational Church.

> *Is Heaven a Physician?*
> *They say that He can heal—*
> *But Medicine Posthumus*
> *Is unavailable—*
> *Is Heaven an Exchequer?*
> *They speak of what we owe—*
> *But that negotiation*
> *I'm not a Party to—*

Edward Dickinson, however, still worried in conventional terms about his daughter's spiritual condition. At last he quieted his anxiety by asking Mr. Jenkins to interview

Emily about her beliefs. No one but Emily and Mr. Jenkins ever knew what was said in that interview, but afterward the minister reported, not without a trace of humor, that he found Emily "sound."

Had she not insisted upon seclusion, Emily Dickinson could not have concentrated on life at a metaphysical level. As it was, her self-made cloister provided her the opportunity to live an original life to fullest capacity. Yet, far from losing interest in the world, she kept track of a multitude of anniversaries and dates significant in the lives of family, friends, and neighbors. When others neglected the anniversary of a birth or death, flowers or a remarkable note from Emily would quietly announce that she remembered.

Amherst sunsets continued to entrance her, as did the changes of light on the Pelham Hills. She watched from her window in the dead of night the surreptitious arrival of a circus. She listened to a boy go whistling by the house. She knew the village news, brought daily from uptown by Vinnie, and the world's news, brought by the *Springfield Republican*. Without leaving home she could conjure up the atmosphere of village social gatherings.

> *The Show is not the Show*
> *But they that go—*
> *Menagerie to me*

My Neighbor be—
Fair Play—
Both went to see—

Everything she saw and read and heard increased her experience and enlarged her knowledge of circumference. At times she was happy, at times despondent, but she was fully occupied, and breathless with the thrill of discovering what life was about. She expressed her ecstatic condition several times in letters to her friends. "To live is so startling, it leaves but little room for other occupations," she proclaimed to Mr. Higginson.

Meanwhile, what of her poems? It is certain Emily Dickinson knew she was a poet, knew she had attained the goal she held supreme. Yet she made no attempt to share her poetry with the world. Her friends knew she wrote poems. Mrs. Holland, Mr. Bowles, Lou and Fanny Norcross, and others all had received Emily's verses enclosed with letters. Dozens of poems had been sent over the path to Sue. Together her friends formed a small, perceptive audience. Although none of them suspected the great volume of Emily's writing, they might be expected to recognize its worth.

To pile like Thunder to it's close
Then crumble grand away

> *While Everything created hid*
> *This—would be Poetry—*

This was one of Emily Dickinson's definitions of poetry. She fulfilled it again and again. Her short, powerful verses, sophisticated in thought, condensed in statement, expressed in lightning-clean phrases, had the effect of leaving a reader breathless with astonishment. But they were decidedly unorthodox by nineteenth-century standards. Mr. Higginson had already pointed out that fact to Emily. It was proved on the rare occasions that one of her poems appeared in print.

Several times Sue or Samuel Bowles arranged the printing of one of Emily's poems in the *Springfield Republican* or some other publication without Emily's knowledge. In each instance, when the poem was published it was changed by a well-intentioned editor to comply with conventions of punctuation, rhyme, or meter. Emily, when she saw her verse, was deeply dismayed.

A further reason the poetry remained unpublished was Emily's scorn for publicity.

> *I'm Nobody! Who are you?*
> *Are you—Nobody—too?*
> *Then there's a pair of us!*
> *Dont tell! they'd banish us—you know!*

How dreary—to be—Somebody!
How public—like a Frog—
To tell your name—the livelong June—
To an admiring Bog!

More importantly, her poetry was an intensely private
matter, part of her most personal experience. If she shared
it at all it was with those who knew the intimate aspects of
her life. She expressed herself emphatically in a poem that
began *"Publication—is the Auction/Of the Mind of
Man,"* and consistently resisted any inducement to publish.

On a sunny, quiet August day in 1870 a handsome,
slightly built gentleman with whiskered chin and gracefully
dignified manner penetrated the tall hedges of the Edward
Dickinson mansion and rang the front door bell. Behind
him the dusty streets of Amherst, reflecting hot afternoon
sun, were nearly empty of people or vehicles.

The great, still brick mansion looked deserted, but in
answer to the gentleman's ring the door was eventually
opened by Maggie. She took Thomas Wentworth Higginson's calling card and showed him into the front parlor, to
the left of the hall. The room was cool and dark, with a
marble mantel and stiff furniture arranged in orderly manner. The whole setting had the reserved appearance of a
time gone by. No profusion of ornaments and knickknacks

fractured the glance. Instead the eye met carefully arranged flowers and a tidy display of books, among which Colonel Higginson noticed his own novel, *Malbone.*

Colonel Higginson had come to the mansion at Emily Dickinson's request. After eight years of irregular correspondence, during which Emily had sent him quite a number of her unusual poems accompanied by pleas for advice and criticism, he had given in to her oft-repeated desire that he visit her in Amherst. Emily had a purpose, she told him. She wanted to thank Mr. Higginson for saving her life.

At first Colonel Higginson, whose literary career kept him extremely busy writing, editing, and lecturing, begged Miss Dickinson to attend one of his many literary meetings.

"You must come down to Boston sometimes?" he urged her. "All ladies do."

"I do not cross my Father's ground to any House or town," Emily replied firmly.

Colonel Higginson's admiration for Emily's poems and letters and his interest in seeing for himself the unconventional woman who wrote them had finally brought him to Amherst. Seated on a small horsehair sofa in the mansion parlor, he noted the book titles, the engravings, the open piano, and waited. Later that evening he described the meeting in a letter to his wife:

"A step like a pattering child's in entry & in glided a little plain woman with two smooth bands of reddish hair & a face a little like Belle Dove's; not plainer—with no good feature—in a very plain & exquisitely clean white pique & a blue net worsted shawl. She came to me with two day lilies which she put in a sort of childlike way into my hand & said 'These are my introduction' in a soft frightened breathless childlike voice—& added under her breath Forgive me if I am frightened; I never see strangers & hardly know what I say—but she talked soon & thenceforward continuously—& differentially—sometimes stopping to ask me to talk instead of her—but readily recommencing."

This word portrait of Emily Dickinson in her fortieth year provides for succeeding generations a rare glimpse of the poet. Emily's remarks, candid and ingenuous, so fascinated Colonel Higginson that he made a list of those he could remember for Mrs. Higginson. But if Emily mentioned just how Mr. Higginson had saved her life when he answered her strange appeal for guidance in 1862, he omitted to record it. Commented Higginson, "I never was with anyone who drained my nerve power so much. Without touching her, she drew from me. I am glad not to live near her."

As a result of their meeting Emily and Colonel Higginson became warmer personal friends. He visited her only once more, three years later, but Emily's letters to the man she chose as preceptor, and whose scholar she always claimed to be, became more familiar and enlarged in subject matter from 1870 onward.

As the pace at which she wrote poetry slowed, letters claimed a greater part of Emily's attention. "A Letter always feels to me like immortality because it is the mind alone without corporeal friend," she wrote to Higginson. She never opened a letter until she had carried it to the privacy of her own room and shut the door. Then she could be alone with the thoughts contained in the envelope.

Letter writing was one of Emily Dickinson's greatest pleasures. She said as much. *"A Letter is a joy of Earth/It is denied the Gods."* Always, from the time she was young, she had taken pride and delight in what she had to say and how she said it. It was an exercise to which she brought all her enjoyment of wit and words, all her skill in manipulating language.

To Ned, who was away at the seashore, she wrote, "The little Turkey is lonely and the Chickens bring him to call. His foreign Neck in familiar Grass is quaint as a Dromedary."

Her warm, humorous observations on life in the Dickinson home were reserved for Lou and Fanny Norcross. "Mother went rambling, and came in with a burdock on her shawl, so we know that the snow has perished from the earth. Noah would have liked mother."

To Colonel Higginson and to Mrs. Holland went her most polished thoughts, some of them so succinct that entire letters were composed of the listing of her terse observations and aphorisms. Such letters were difficult to read, as much for the illegible scrawl in which Emily wrote as for her compact messages.

Rarely did she write a letter or note without first composing a rough draft. This she worked over, changing a word here, adding one there, until satisfaction came. On paper she could control the thoughts and emotions which so easily ran away with her during personal confrontations. While she was engrossed in other occupations a line of prose might spring into Emily's head. Quickly, so as not to lose it, she would write down the inspiration on the margin of her newspaper, on the reverse of a grocery list, on any of the handy scraps of paper a New England household was reluctant to throw away.

Once in a great while a phrase so pleased her that she included it in letters to more than one person. But she wrote in such distinct styles to different friends that the same thought rarely fitted two individuals.

Life in the Dickinson home had changed little in its essential features since the time Emily was young. The family circle, which was her refuge, was still unbroken. At forty Emily Dickinson lived among people she had always known and loved and whose personalities were as familiar as the sun that rose and set each day.

Vinnie, also approaching forty years of age, was proud and protective of her gifted sister. Vinnie had never married. She was no longer pretty. Her black hair was parted and pulled back behind her head in very plain fashion, her features were strong and angular. Clever in her own right, Vinnie had developed a tongue so sharp that people called at the mansion to be entertained by her funny but vitriolic remarks.

The sisters complemented one another. Vinnie took care of practical matters, freeing Emily for more ethereal pursuits. The younger sister addressed the elder's letters and packages, saw to the delivery of notes and the bouquets Emily arranged. When a dressmaker was called in to make one of Emily's simple white frocks, she fitted the garment to Vinnie, who was the same size. The sisters favored dress styles they had worn as young women, styles that looked a bit outdated in the 1870's.

Emily easily gave way to her sister's strongly voiced opinions on worldly matters. If Vinnie's chief failing took the form of love of cats, so that a constant parade of pussies and their offspring inhabited the mansion, it was to be borne. Emily could poke kindly fun at Vinnie's concern over the trials and tribulations of her feline menagerie, but she was much too fond of birds to do more than tolerate the creatures.

Austin and Sue were perhaps more perceptive in their appreciation of Emily's unique abilities than other members of the family. Austin shared his sister's sensitivity to the beauties of nature. His love of trees and shrubs, which was reflected in the handsome plantings around his home, had led him to organize the reclamation of the long-unsightly town common. At his direction the swampy areas were filled, the ground evened and the whole tract planted with elms.

Austin was slightly less the prominent citizen his father was in Amherst, but he was more generally beloved. While his ringing command could cause a small boy who had neglected to close the garden gate to tremble in his boots, he was a sympathetic man, kindly and grave, who was consulted by the townspeople on matters significant and insignificant. He was a central figure in First Church affairs, and for many years served as town-meeting moderator. Emily and Vinnie still looked to their brother for advice and support, and in turn he frequented the mansion so regularly that at times it seemed as if he had never left home.

The affection Sue and Emily had had for one another during girlhood had strengthened throughout the years shared as sisters-in-law. Sue, who was Emily's antithesis in almost every aspect but intellect, was a strong, handsome woman, bitingly witty and outspoken. She had established herself as Amherst's leading hostess at a time when the town's social life was growing very active. The college was prospering. New people with new ways were moving to Amherst. Dinner parties and receptions had become more frequent and more elaborate than in previous decades. Sue entered energetically into the stepped-up social pace, and her high-handed, commanding, and sometimes insincere ways earned her the admiration of some, the intense dislike of others.

Kept busy by her children, her social activities, and the running of a large household, Sue at times saw little of Emily. The two kept in touch by way of notes sent back and forth between their homes, with Ned and Mattie acting as messengers. Occasionally the equally determined personalities saw oppositely and they quarreled. Most often the notes still in existence attest to a strong bond of love and admiration that existed between them.

The Dickinson who played the least influential role in Emily's life was her mother. In fact, it is difficult to keep in mind that Mrs. Dickinson was an active member of the family, for unless she was undergoing a bout of illness, Emily made little mention of her in letters. "My Mother does not care for thought," was the brief introduction accorded her in an early letter to Mr. Higginson, and it undoubtedly serves as explanation for why mother and daughter were not close.

Mrs. Dickinson's concerns were the many duties that kept the household running, the dozens of trifling matters that daily bid for attention. Visitors found her conversation parochial, often exasperatingly limited to whether a guest was warm enough, cool enough, comfortable enough in one chair or another. Mrs. Dickinson was not the parent who represented protection and security to Emily.

As ever, the dominant figure in the family was Father. In his seventies Edward Dickinson was still fierce of countenance, still stern and unbending in character. Household routine revolved around his comings and goings, his wishes, the little attentions he preferred. If the members of the family felt no closer to penetrating his formidable reserve, they perhaps loved him all the more deeply for appreciating the terrible control his puritanical convictions held over his heart and soul.

In 1872 Squire Dickinson at last, after thirty-seven years, retired from his position as treasurer of Amherst College. He was pleased to be succeeded in the duty by Austin. Still acknowledged the town's most distinguished citizen, the Squire had nevertheless come to be considered a bit old-fashioned. Times had changed. Edward Dickinson's political views were outdated. More and more frequently he was politely referred to as "a gentleman of the elder school." Yet, in 1873, when Hampshire County needed a strong representative to go to the state legislature to fight for bringing a section of the Vermont Central Railway to the region, Squire Dickinson was elected.

The portrait of Edward Dickinson as a strict, unsympathetic, duty-bound New Englander is occasionally relieved by the observations of his elder daughter. Emily could see in her father the slightly comical figure who stepped like Cromwell as he fetched shavings for the fireplace, or the secretly gentle man who went into the snow in his slippers to scatter crumbs for hungry birds, then hid himself in order not to cause the tiny creatures embarrassment.

One warm early summer afternoon in 1874 when Edward Dickinson was home for a weekend lull between meetings of the legislature, Emily devoted a few hours she usually reserved for herself to being with her father. The two shared the time quietly but so enjoyably that Father almost embarrassed Emily by actually stating he would like the afternoon not to end.

Two days later the family was shattered by the news, sent by telegraph from Boston, that Edward Dickinson was dead. That he had died alone in strange surroundings distressed the Dickinsons, that he died while carrying out his duty, following a speech in the legislature, surprised no one.

Austin was most stunned of all the family by his

father's death, and afterward could remember little about the funeral, not even who had carried the coffin to the grave-yard. Emily took her grief to her room where she sat alone and admitted no one but Samuel Bowles. Mr. Bowles came at once from Springfield and took charge of funeral arrangements. Mrs. Dickinson was helpless, but Vinnie rallied to assist Mr. Bowles, and Sue arranged a wreath of white daisies from the Dickinson meadow, the only flowers to adorn the austere figure in the coffin.

The town mourned the passing of its great citizen, and on the afternoon of the funeral, stores closed and the citizens of Amherst came to fill the settees brought from the college and lined up in the Dickinson parlor, the front hall, and on the lawn outside the mansion. Those outdoors could not hope to hear the hymn, the Scripture reading, and the single prayer spoken by the Reverend Mr. Jenkins, but they came out of respect and sat breathing the heavy funereal odor of blooming syringa, sharing the general sorrow.

It was many, many months before Emily was reconciled to her father's disappearance from earth. She missed him on so many levels of her being that she could only pursue with relentless questioning and probing what had happened to the pure and terrible heart that had been a mainstay of her existence. Her life was dated by the day her father died, so that she counted time by its passage from June

16, 1874. It marked a renewal of her intimate acquaintance with death. A year later Emily crowned her father's memory and her own genius with a poem.

> *Lay this Laurel on the One*
> *Too intrinsic for Renown—*
> *Laurel—vail your deathless tree—*
> *Him you chasten, that is He!*

$Seven$

My life closed twice before its close;
It yet remains to see
If Immortality unveil
A third event to me,

So huge, so hopeless to conceive
As these that twice befel.
Parting is all we know of heaven,
And all we need of hell.

It is not possible to know when Emily Dickinson wrote this poem. The two shattering events to which she refers are

not identified. But possibly the verse was composed following that "first Mystery of the House," her father's death.

More than two years after Edward Dickinson's funeral
Emily admitted, "I dream about father every night, always
a different dream, and forget what I am doing daytimes,
wondering where he is. Without any body, I keep thinking.
What kind can that be?"

Each time she passed his door in the narrow, shadowed
upstairs hall of the mansion she agonized anew. Once the
door had represented safety. Now there was only the unknown, the haunting, unanswered questions. Emily's mind
explored them endlessly. Her tremulous "where is he?" was
remembered by her brother's children even after they were
grown.

Were it not for death, said Emily, there would be no want
of heaven, for life on earth was heaven enough. Except for
the "Balmless Wound" left by departed loved ones, life was
to her a state of supreme happiness, a joyful experience. Her
ecstasy in being alive, what she called glee intuitive, was
communicated with love to those whom she held dear. Yet
in the midst of life there was death, and the attempt to
reconcile one experience with the other at times seemed
superhuman.

By the Christmas following her father's death Emily had
recovered her spirits enough that she could bring gentle
humor to the task of thanking cousins for a wreath sent for

the Squire's grave. The cousins would never have dared give Father a Christmas present when he was alive, suggested Emily, for they knew how "he frowned upon Santa Claus— and all such prowling gentlemen."

Edward Dickinson's death signaled the collapse of a demure life long dependent upon his. As if reacting to the absence of the powerful will that had so long dominated the household, Mrs. Dickinson one year later suffered a stroke that left her a bedridden, partly paralyzed invalid.

Her illness changed the lives of Emily and Lavinia, who for the next seven years became her devoted nursemaids. It was nearly a full-time occupation. "To read to her, to fan her, to tell her health will come tomorrow, to explain to her *why* the grasshopper is a burden, because he is not so new a grasshopper as he was,—this is so ensuing, I hardly have said 'Good-morning, mother,' when I hear myself saying, 'Mother, good-night.'"

In addition, Emily planned the sick-room meals, cooking special dishes to tempt her mother's faded appetite. Emily's delicate notes thanked neighbors for thoughtful gifts of fruit and flowers brought to the ailing patient.

And amazingly, as time passed, a curious change took place in the relationship of mother and daughter. Mrs. Dickinson's lack of interest in thought and conversation had always stood in the way of any real intimacy between herself and her elder daughter. So muted a role had Mrs.

Dickinson played in Emily's unusual life that Emily had shocked Colonel Higginson once by musing, "I never had a mother. I suppose a mother is one to whom you hurry when you are troubled." Mrs. Dickinson could scarcely have understood the things that troubled Emily.

Yet, as Emily tended the invalid's little wants, soothed her pain, eased her wandering mind, she came to love her mother as one loves a helpless, dependent child. Tenderness and affection grew. When Mrs. Dickinson finally died late in 1882, Emily realized, "a larger mother died than had she died before."

But sorrow and upheaval compete in life with bliss, and such a joyful event as the birth of another child to Austin and Sue in 1875 could soothe an aching spirit. The baby was a second boy. He was named Gilbert, and always called Gib.

From the time he was old enough to run outdoors, Emily began to know and love Gib. She watched him playing in a tub of water in the driveway, rejoiced to see the "little Missionary" doing neighborhood errands with a basket on his arm. His secrets delighted her, as did his cry, "Don't tell, Aunt Emily!" Adored by all the Dickinsons, Gib formed a loving link between the two houses.

"Were'nt you chasing Pussy?" Aunt Vinnie accused the little boy one day, seeing one of her precious cats shooting past the kitchen door.

"No," came the innocent answer. "She was chasing herself."

"But was'nt she running pretty fast?" persisted Vinnie.

"Well, some slow and some fast," was Gib's explanation.

Emily laughed until her sides ached, and reached for paper and pencil to describe the incident for Sue.

Emily enjoyed watching Ned and Mattie grow up, too. Ned was fourteen when Gib was born. The older boy was very fond of his Aunt Emily, with whom he found he could talk over many problems he didn't care to mention to his family. The two shared a love for the books of Charles Dickens and joked together in a private language based on characters from the English novels. When Ned reached an age where he began questioning the faith of his fathers, he found his aunt a sympathetic person with whom to discuss his uncertainties.

Through her niece, Emily Dickinson was reminded of the friendships and pastimes of her own childhood. Fondly she watched Mattie and her best friend, Did Jenkins, playing with their dolls under the shrubbery, rolling their hoops through crackling fall leaves, dressing in their mothers' cast-off finery to pay calls on the neighborhood. Amused by the ups and downs of the young friendship, Emily could not refrain from sometimes sending them little notes.

In 1877, to the distress of all the Dickinsons, Mr. Jenkins left the Amherst church to take a pulpit in Pittsfield, fifty miles away. Despite separation, the Dickinson and Jenkins families remained friends, and Mattie and Did paid one another annual visits.

At sixteen Mattie sat for some photograph portraits. One picture was taken with her hat on, one with her hat off. Aunt Emily saw the former. When she sent the portrait back to the other house by way of Gib, she inscribed an exultant note to Mattie. "That's the Little Girl I always meant to be, but was'nt— The very Hat I always meant to wear, but did'nt and the attitude toward the Universe, so precisely my own, that I feel very much, as if I were returning Elisha's Horses, or the Vision of John at Patmos—"

Early in 1878 a sorrowful event took place. The beloved friend of all the Dickinsons, Samuel Bowles, died after prolonged and serious illness in his Springfield home. When the news reached Amherst Emily took up her pen to write a few brokenhearted words to his widow. "To remember our own Mr. Bowles is all we can do. With grief it is done, so warmly and long, it can never be new. Emily."

Never again would there be that sweet anticipation, that special flurry of excitement that precipitated Sam Bowles's arrival in Amherst. Each of the Dickinsons had his own fond memories of the Springfield editor. A "certain Slant of light" that tinted the Pelham hills purple toward the close of mid-winter days brought him to mind. He had loved the lavender. Emily could smile about the time she sent a note downstairs from her room saying she could not possibly see Mr. Bowles on that particular occasion.

Samuel Bowles read the note, rose at once from his chair, and bounded several paces up the front stairs.

"Emily, you damned rascal!" he called out severely. "No more of this nonsense! I've traveled all the way from Springfield to see you. Come down at once."

To the utter amazement of Vinnie and Austin, their sister came down at once, her eyes sparkling with fun. No one but Sam Bowles would have gotten away with it.

If ever immortality was represented on earth it was in the person of Samuel Bowles, Emily felt. She once told him, "You have the most triumphant Face out of Paradise— probably because you are there constantly, instead of ultimately—" After his death she comforted those who mourned him with the same thought.

The deaths of her father and Mr. Bowles seemed to strengthen the poet's belief in immortality. "We are eternal —dear," she wrote to a friend who had lost her husband, "which seems so worthless, now—but will be by and by, all we can remember—because it owns our own and must give them back—"

But what eternity was, and in what form one came to know it, were the unanswered and unanswerable questions. "I believe we shall in some manner be cherished by our Maker—that the One who gave us this remarkable earth has the power still farther to surprise that which He has caused. Beyond that all is silence." Yet the desire to know never ceased nagging Emily's soul.

Other experiences shared her mind with immortality, and one especially brought great joy into her life. When she was forty-seven years old she again fell in love. This time the affection was returned.

Judge Otis Phillips Lord had been for years one of Edward Dickinson's closest friends. Almost twenty years older than Emily, the judge had had an outstanding career as lawyer, state legislator, and judge of the state superior court. Now he was a judge of the state supreme court. Emily had always known him, for with his wife Judge Lord had visited the Dickinson home frequently. Sometime after Mrs. Lord's death in 1877, Emily and Otis Lord realized their mutual affection.

The relationship brought Emily great happiness. A note of joyousness crept into her letters to others than Judge Lord, and she admitted that loving him made a difference that affected all she did.

Judge Lord came to Amherst periodically to see Emily, staying for several weeks at a time at the hotel. Between times Emily wrote long, ecstatic letters to him at his home in Salem. Although she contemplated becoming his wife, within a very few years the possibility of such a drastic change was forestalled by Judge Lord's increasing ill-health.

The occasions upon which Emily Dickinson saw outsiders had become now extremely rare. One was etched on the memories of two young Amherst girls, Nora and Clara Green, who on a certain sunny June morning received a note from Lavinia Dickinson asking them to come to the mansion.

Nora Green had, a short time before, sung a solo during the farewell service for Mr. Jenkins. Lavinia had heard her sing and had praised the performance so highly that Emily wished to hear it too. Would Nora sing for Miss Emily that evening, asked Miss Lavinia? Nora sent word that she would.

After supper, Nora, her sister, and her brother, Nelson, walked up Main Street together. Their excitement increased with every step.

"What do you suppose she'll look like?" ventured Nelson. "All in white, of course."

"Tiny, too, I hear. With lovely hair," added Clara in a low voice.

"Once there was a lover, you know," embroidered Nelson, remembering a story he had heard several times. "But old Squire Dickinson kept them from marrying. There was a big fuss. Miss Emily swore never to set foot out the front door again."

"Nelson, hush!" said Nora with unusual severity. She had been very quiet during their walk, her usually buoyant spirits subdued by a sense of awe at being called to see Miss Emily. No one she knew had seen Emily Dickinson for years. Some in Amherst even called her a myth.

The three turned in at the break in the Dickinson hedge, pushed through the gate and climbed the front steps. Miss Lavinia was watching for them. She opened the big front door before the children could ring the bell and promptly ushered them into the parlor. The windows stood open, their light summer drapes swaying in the warm evening breeze.

"I'll go up to my sister to tell her you're ready to sing," said Lavinia, waving her hand vaguely toward the upright piano at the far side of the room. "We'll be able to hear you perfectly."

Nora was dumbfounded. She looked at Clara, whose surprise showed in her face, and at Nelson, with his mouth ajar.

Then there was to be no audience after all! They would not see Miss Emily. Nora was terribly disappointed. Followed by her brother and sister she went to the piano. She waited until Miss Lavinia's feet had stopped sounding on the stairs. Pressing one of the instrument's keys for pitch, Nora began singing the first phrases of the Twenty-third Psalm in her lovely soprano.

When it was over and the room was silent again, the children could hear a faint clapping sound fluttering down

the stairway. It was followed by Miss Lavinia, who returned
to the parlor.

"Emily would like to thank you herself," Vinnie said to
Nora. "Will you and your sister come with me?"

Nora and Clara followed Miss Lavinia across the front
hall into the dim library. The curtains were drawn. A little
of the lingering daylight filtered through the cracks. Suddenly a tiny figure in white darted into the room and took
their hands in her small grasp.

"I cannot thank you," she said rapidly, in her lilting,
breathless voice. "Except for the birds yours is the first song
I have heard in many years."

While the girls gazed at her, gaining an impression of
large, dark eyes set in a tiny, precise face, Emily quickly
told them how she had loved the piano, but finally stopped
playing because she was convinced she would never be
an artist.

She said a few things more and then was gone. Nora and
Clara found Nelson waiting on the doorstep, said good-bye
to Miss Lavinia, and started home to recount an experience
neither girl would ever forget.

Another unusual interview took place in the autumn of
1878, when Mrs. Helen Hunt Jackson came to call on Emily
Dickinson. Mrs. Jackson was a former Amherst girl, the
widow of the Major Hunt Emily had so enjoyed meeting
that commencement nearly two decades earlier. She had

become one of the most popular women authors in America. Using the initials H.H. as pen name, Helen Hunt Jackson had written several novels and a widely acclaimed volume of verse. Although she had long been away from Amherst and was a few years older than Emily Dickinson, the two had known one another slightly during girlhood.

Mrs. Jackson was also a literary friend of Thomas Wentworth Higginson's. He had shown her some of the strange poems Emily Dickinson wrote, and Helen Hunt Jackson thought them marvelous. Several times she wrote Emily begging her to publish. Emily always said no.

In 1878 Mrs. Jackson was helping a Boston publisher compile material for an unusual book. Called *A Masque of Poets,* the book was to contain unsigned verses that noted American poets had written but never before published. Readers were to have the fun of guessing who the authors of the anonymous verses could be. John Greenleaf Whittier had agreed to give a poem. So had Ralph Waldo Emerson and Louisa May Alcott and many others, including H.H. herself. Mrs. Jackson was determined Emily Dickinson should be represented too.

Finding she could not persuade Emily by way of letters, Mrs. Jackson at last, while on a trip to New England, came to call. That autumn morning, while Mattie hopped excitedly up and down the path outside the hedges, thrilled at seeing the famous H.H. sweep up the mansion's front steps, and while the Dickinsons' hired man walked the Jackson carriage horses up and down the road, the two women met and talked for an hour.

They were very different, Emily Dickinson and Helen Hunt Jackson. The latter was a plump woman, outgoing, worldly, spontaneous, and indomitable. She charmed almost all she met. She charmed Emily as well, although Mrs. Jackson's own comment, that their differences made her feel like a great ox talking to a moth, seems very apt.

Emily did not give in to Mrs. Jackson's request that morning, but evidently did a short time later. When *A Masque of Poets* appeared in mid-November it contained Emily Dickinson's poem "Success is counted sweetest." A word added here, three words changed there, but otherwise Emily's.

The two ladies, each a confessed admirer of the other, continued to correspond from time to time. Emily sent several poems to her friend. Mrs. Jackson praised them all, but no more appeared in print.

A visit even more momentous for Emily Dickinson took place during a summer evening in 1880. With no forewarning the Reverend Charles Wadsworth called to see her. They had not met for twenty years. Although there is evidence that Emily wrote to Wadsworth many times after his return in 1870 from California to Philadelphia, none of the correspondence survives. We can only surmise she asked

Wadsworth her many questions about the unknown, that realm which was to her "the largest need of the intellect."

Popular authors and Philadelphia ministers did not call every day, however. The peaceful routine within the Dickinson mansion was usually interrupted only by those small intrusions Emily claimed taught her about life. The occupations of her heart and mind changed little. Five years after her father's death Emily still listed that and the death of Bowles and the illness of her mother as the events that unceasingly preoccupied her.

Emily shared most of her daytime hours with her sister. Together, with Maggie's help, they cared for the house as it had been cared for when Squire Dickinson was alive. Vinnie was constantly in motion, now charging away at some formidable household task, now proclaiming to Emily and Maggie her opinions on matters great and small. Emily claimed she could know no fear with such a sister.

Vinnie took seriously her role of guardian of the more timid Emily. Her overzealous attempt to keep Emily from knowledge of near-disaster during Amherst's worst fire, which occurred in the predawn hours of July 4, 1879, is amusingly described by Emily herself in a letter to Lou and Fanny Norcross.

"We were waked by the ticking of the bells,—the bells tick in Amherst for a fire, to tell the firemen.

"I sprang to the window, and each side of the curtain saw that awful sun. The moon was shining high at the time, and the birds singing like trumpets.

"Vinnie came soft as a moccasin, 'Don't be afraid, Emily, it is only the fourth of July.'

"I did not tell that I saw it, for I thought if she felt it best to deceive, it must be that it was.

"She took hold of my hand and led me into mother's room. Mother had not waked, and Maggie was sitting by her. Vinnie left us a moment, and I whispered to Maggie, and asked her what it was.

" 'Only Stebbins's barn, Emily;' but I knew that the right and left of the village was on the arm of Stebbins's barn. I could hear buildings falling, and oil exploding, and people walking and talking gayly, and cannon soft as velvet from parishes that did not know that we were burning up.

"And so much lighter than day was it, that I saw a caterpillar measure a leaf far down in the orchard; and Vinnie kept saying bravely, 'It's only the fourth of July.'

"It seemed like a theatre, or a night in London, or perhaps like chaos. The innocent dew falling 'as

if it thought no evil,' . . . and sweet frogs prattling
in the pools as if there were no earth.

"At seven people came to tell us that the fire was
stopped, stopped by throwing sound houses in as one
fills a well.

"Mother never waked, and we were all grateful; we
knew she would never buy needle and thread at Mr. Cutler's
store, and if it were Pompeii nobody could tell her. . . .

"Vinnie's 'only the fourth of July' I shall always
remember. I think she will tell us so when we die,
to keep us from being afraid."

*"Parting is all we know of Heaven, / And all we need of
hell,"* she had written. No more apt words could preface the
final few years of Emily Dickinson's life.

She had reached the age of fifty by 1881, and had lost
only a few of the persons dearest to her. "My friends are my
'estate'," she once told Bowles. "Forgive me then the avarice
to hoard them!" Within the next few years more of those
friends than Emily could bear to lose escaped her. Each loss
rent a large hole in the fabric of her emotional life.

The death on April 1, 1882, of the Reverend Charles
Wadsworth was the first loss, and an anguish she could
share with no one. The other Dickinsons had not known

him. Emily herself knew next to nothing about his private life, for their relationship had been sustained by spiritual concerns. Her Shepherd, she called him. His portrait had hung on the wall of her room for many years. His sermons, published from time to time, she had read avidly. Shaken by Wadsworth's dying, Emily sought outside help to still an ancient, nagging doubt that beset her unmercifully in times of distress. "Is immortality true?" she queried in a letter to a prominent Springfield clergyman whose name she had read in the newspaper.

Six months after Wadsworth's death Mrs. Dickinson's life came to an end. She died easily and swiftly one November morning with her daughters nearby. "The dear Mother that could not walk, has *flown*," wrote Emily with sad surprise. She missed the precious burden as she could not have conceived of doing a decade earlier.

The relationship between the Austin Dickinson home and the mansion had known periods of great strain since the death of Edward Dickinson. Although the tensions were never specifically mentioned in letters, that they existed is noticeable in some of the surviving notes that passed from Emily to her sister-in-law. It seems likely that Vinnie and Sue, both strong-willed and opinionated, were not compatible.

Emily's own love for Sister Sue, whom years before she had welcomed so eagerly into the family, never entirely dissolved. While far from blind to Susan's faults, Emily kept faithful to a slender tie that united their very different natures. The love held in common for Austin and Sue's children, and in particular for Gib, kept the tempers of the two households within reasonable control. When, during the autumn he was eight years old, Gib contracted typhoid fever and after a few days' severe illness died, the event was almost too much for any of the Dickinsons to bear.

The death of little Gib was the one that completely stunned Emily. She never became reconciled to it and for the rest of her life could not bear to talk about it, although it weighed constantly on her heart.

Stricken by nervous prostration after Gib died, Emily was ill for many weeks. She recovered her health slowly during the winter months that followed. Sitting in her room, with hyacinths and carnations filling her four window sills, Emily worked intermittently at the one occupation that still commanded all her powers, writing poetry. Small wonder that the poems were brief and fragmentary and almost all were elegies.

In March of 1884 Judge Lord died at his home in Salem. Emily had emotional strength left to summon outraged grief that she should be deprived of her greatest consolation.

> *So give me back to Death—*
> *The Death I never feared*

Except that it deprived of thee—
And now, by Life deprived,
In my own Grave I breathe
And estimate it's size—
It's size is all that Hell can guess—
And all that Heaven was—

Emily's own final illness, Bright's disease, came upon her periodically during the last two years of her life. It was complicated by the emotional distress she had undergone. "The Dyings have been too deep for me, and before I could raise my Heart from one, another has come—" she wrote a friend.

One more death saddened her, that of her friend Helen Hunt Jackson in the summer of 1885. Shocked as well as saddened, for Emily Dickinson had been corresponding with Mrs. Jackson and had recently been assured by the author herself of her good health.

Helen Hunt Jackson was the single person who consistently spoke unqualified praise of Emily Dickinson's poetry. The year before dying, Mrs. Jackson had also asked Emily for the right to take charge of the unpublished verse, should she outlive Emily. Emily did not answer, and Mrs. Jackson did not live the longer.

The hundreds of verses lay in varying stages of completion within the bottom drawer of the poet's bureau. There were the hand-sewn booklets containing about a thousand poems Emily considered finished. There, too, were the worksheets, the rough drafts, the fragments of hundreds of other poems and of many, many letters. Single thoughts scrawled on torn bits of paper, verses with lists of words awaiting substitution, unsuccessful poems needing eventual reworking, all together with the priceless hoard of completed poetry. Nothing dated, nothing titled, little organized, but every scrap too valuable to throw away. This was Emily Dickinson's "letter to the world."

The message of her letter is said a thousand ways, each a testimonial of rejoicing to that incredible quality called life. "It is strange that the Astounding subjects are the only ones we pass unmoved," she had written. She was an exception to this, for she had dedicated her lifetime and her genius to exploring the giant themes most humans find so easy to avoid.

She had not found the answers, had found instead that maturity brought only greater complexity. *"The Spirit lasts—but in what mode—"* was the perplexing question she still asked after a lifetime's study of the Astounding subjects. But her discovered province was the radiant joy of being, the condition she called ecstasy. Almost her last poem, written after she had survived the deaths of one friend after another, miraculously confirms her undiminished sense of ecstasy.

Take all away from me, but leave me Ecstasy,
And I am richer then than all my Fellow Men—
Ill it becometh me to dwell so wealthily
When at my very Door are those possessing more,
In abject poverty—

True to her intention of years before, she had explored life, and discovered that its size approximated the dimensions of the human heart. Personal timidity obscured the boldness of her undertaking, seclusion belied the breadth of her experience. To the eyes she could not see she bequeathed her knowledge. She had accomplished her mission as a poet.

The Poets light but Lamps—
Themselves—go out—
The Wicks they stimulate—
If vital Light

Inhere as do the Suns—
Each Age a Lens
Disseminating their
Circumference—

The long romance with life and language and literature was over. In May of 1886 Emily Dickinson succumbed to a final attack of Bright's disease. She died late in the afternoon of May 15, with Austin and Vinnie close by, as they had always been.

Those who attended her funeral commented upon its remarkable and fitting beauty. The day was dazzlingly clear and warm and sunny. Emily's white coffin, covered with violets and ground pine, lay on a special bier in the Dickinson parlor. A few people gathered. Thomas Wentworth Higginson had come from Cambridge to read a favorite poem of Emily Dickinson's, "Immortality" by Emily Brontë. Mr. Jenkins had come from Pittsfield to say a prayer. When he finished, the honorary pallbearers, among them the president of Amherst College, carried the casket out the back door of the mansion into the sunshine. There six men, all of whom at one time or another had been workmen on the Dickinson grounds, shouldered the burden and carried it the back way across the fields to West Cemetery. Following along the narrow footpath, which threaded the thick, wild grass and swaying buttercups, came a few friends and neighbors.

Several days later, Vinnie, beginning the sad task of sorting through Emily's possessions, opened the bottom drawer of her sister's cherry bureau and found the poems.

Reading List

The following books about
Emily Dickinson provide interesting and enjoyable reading,
as well as supplementary information and differing opinions
about this endlessly fascinating poet.

Ancestors' Brocades by Millicent Todd Bingham. New
York, Harper & Brothers, 1945. An account of the gradual publication of Emily Dickinson's poetry.

*Dear Preceptor: The Life and Times of Thomas Went-
worth Higginson* by Anna Mary Wells. Boston,
Houghton Mifflin Company, 1963.

Emily Dickinson, An Interpretive Biography by Thomas
H. Johnson. Cambridge, The Belknap Press of Harvard
University Press, 1955.

Emily Dickinson, Face to Face by Martha Dickinson Bian-
chi. Boston, Houghton Mifflin Company, 1932. Notes
and reminiscences of Emily Dickinson and her environment by her niece, Mattie.

Emily Dickinson, Friend and Neighbor by MacGregor
Jenkins. Boston, Little, Brown and Company, 1930.

Memories of boyhood relationships with the poet and the Dickinson families.

Emily Dickinson's Home by Millicent Todd Bingham. New York, Harper & Brothers, 1955. Letters of Edward Dickinson and his family, with documentation and comment by Mrs. Bingham.

Final Harvest, Emily Dickinson's poems selected and introduced by Thomas H. Johnson. Boston, Little, Brown and Company, 1962.

Poems of Emily Dickinson, selected by Helen Plotz. New York, Thomas Y. Crowell Company, 1964.

Remembrance of Amherst: An Undergraduate's Diary 1846–1848 edited by George F. Whicher. New York, Columbia University Press, 1946. The diary kept by William Gardiner Hammond, a graduate of Amherst College in 1848, gives a glimpse into the Amherst of Emily Dickinson's girlhood.

The Capsule of the Mind by Theodora Ward. Cambridge, The Belknap Press of Harvard University Press, 1961. Six essays about Emily Dickinson's poetry.

The Letters of Emily Dickinson, edited by Thomas H. Johnson, associate editor Theodora Ward. Cambridge, The Belknap Press of Harvard University Press, 1958, 3 vols. The complete, annotated collection of Emily Dickinson's correspondence.

The Years and Hours of Emily Dickinson, by Jay Leyda.

New Haven, Yale University Press, 1960, 2 vols. A chronology of events touching the lives of Emily Dickinson and her family.

This Was a Poet by George F. Whicher. New York, Charles Scribner's Sons, 1938. A biography of Emily Dickinson.

Index

About the Author

Polly Ormsby Longsworth grew up in Waterford, a small town in upstate New York. She was graduated from Emma Willard School in Troy, New York, and from Smith College.

When her husband became assistant to the president of Amherst College, the Longsworths moved to Massachusetts. There Mrs. Longsworth fell under the spell of Emily Dickinson, and she began writing this biography of the exquisite poet who drew what was purest and most enduring from the Puritan tradition and her Amherst environment.